P9-BXZ-723

The Design Cookbook
Recipes for a Stylish Home

KELLY EDWARDS

MEDALLION
PRESS

DEDICATION

To Mom, my biggest fan. Without you, all those ladies at the grocery stores across America would never know I'm your daughter. I love you.

To Dad. Your creative spirit, endless love, and support are more than any daughter could ever ask for. If it weren't for you, this book wouldn't even exist. I love you.

Published 2013 by Medallion Press, Inc.
The MEDALLION PRESS LOGO
is a registered trademark of Medallion Press, Inc.

If you purchase this book without a cover, you should be aware that this book is stolen property. It was reported as "unsold and destroyed" to the publisher, and neither the author nor the publisher has received any payment for this "stripped book."

Copyright © 2013 by Kelly Edwards
Written by Kelly Edwards
Art Direction by James Tampa
Edited by Emily Steele
Formatting by Michal Wlos
Cover Photos by Eric Curtis (front) and Brian Lahiere (back)

All rights reserved. No part of this book may be reproduced or transmitted in any form or by any electronic or mechanical means, including photocopying, recording, or by any information storage and retrieval system, without written permission of the publisher, except where permitted by law.

Typeset in Avenir and Gentium

ISBN # 978-160542532-0
10 9 8 7 6 5 4 3 2 1

First Edition
medallionmediagroup.com

ACKNOWLEDGMENTS

Brian Lahiere, I'm not sure what to thank you for the most—your amazing photography or your never-ending patience. You're the most patient man I've ever met. I love you with my whole heart.

Casandra Franceschi, thank you for taking this journey with me. I couldn't have done this without you. You always have faith and the ability to smooth out the wrinkles. I love you for that.

Michael Psaltis, you are a wonderful book agent. I'm going to miss calling you all the time for your helpful advice and direction. It was your guidance and words of wisdom that made all this happen. Hopefully we can do this again!

Vanessa Kogevinas, thank you for fielding the endless phone calls, e-mails, spreadsheets, and photographs that came across your desk. You kept me organized and balanced. That is more of a gift than you will ever know.

Elizabeth Kell Sheinkopf, you're the best editor on planet earth and the greatest friend. Now let's go out and celebrate, shall we?

Jen Porter, your heart is even bigger than your home. Thank you for opening up both to me. I couldn't have picked a better kitchen for the cover.

To Brigitte Johnson-Shepard for introducing and welcoming me into the Medallion Press family. Thank you all for believing in this project!

Thank you to Yui Sugano and Brie Sausser for being all-hands-on-deck.

To Behr, Algami Glass, Mission Tile, Pergo, Flor, Halstead International, Allure Flooring, Top Stone Countertops, Calypso Home, and HP Wall Art for donating products and labor to make this book happen.

To my friends and family who listened, loved, and encouraged me throughout this process. You all know who you are. May there be a lot more dance parties in our future!

Mom and Dad, thank you for all your love and support. I'm proud to be your daughter.

And last but not least, to all the designers and photographers who contributed to this book. You're truly an inspiration to me!

TABLE OF CONTENTS

INTRODUCTION

For me, designing a space is so rewarding. It allows me to be creative and come up with new and innovative ideas every day. From the colors to the textures, I love to see it all come together in the end. I also love the fact that design is really just a game of trial and error. You can take your time, figure out what you like, play with variations of colors and styles, and ultimately create something you're proud of.

Lucky for me, my first job was on HGTV's *Design on a Dime*, where the phrase *trial and error* was an understatement. After all, with a thousand dollars to do a room, we were constantly being challenged! I was also privileged to grow up in a house with a very handy father and brother, who could literally build a house from scratch. They taught me with a little bit of patience and elbow grease, you can always bring a project together—one way or another.

When deciding what kind of design book I wanted to write, I gravitated toward what I'm good at: visualizing and creating things. But instead of embarking on the typical DIY guide for the budget conscious or the coffee table picture book showcasing the most amazing places you've ever seen, I took inspiration from cookbooks, adding something for everybody.

Cookbooks are easy to read with their step-by-step approach. By simply following the directions, you can create something amazing that everyone will take notice of. That's how I wanted this book to feel as well.

I hope you will use this book as your inspirational guide to creating a home you love and are proud of. Whether you have fifty or fifty thousand dollars, here's to designing a space you look forward to coming home to every day!

Cheers!

Kelly

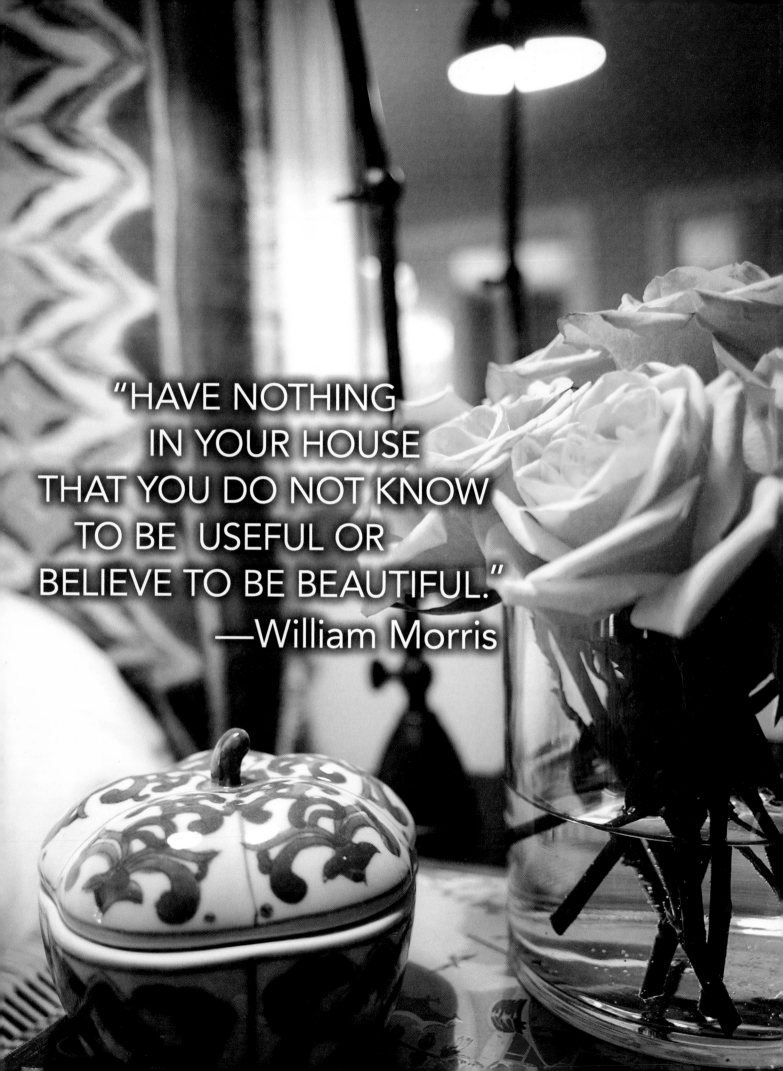

"HAVE NOTHING
IN YOUR HOUSE
THAT YOU DO NOT KNOW
TO BE USEFUL OR
BELIEVE TO BE BEAUTIFUL."
—William Morris

DEFINING YOUR STYLE

- Think of how you want to live and feel. Pull tear sheets from books, magazines, or online. Collect paint swatches and pieces of fabric that reflect how you aspire to live. Put it on a board or in a folder and you'll start to see the bigger picture and be able to more appropriately define your style.

- Establish a style in your home that reflects who you are and where you've been. The easiest way to do this is to pull five things from your home that you genuinely gravitate toward. Incorporating things that are personal to you—your vase collection, travel photos, your grandmother's china, or the luxe linens you can't do without—will ultimately present you with a design road map to a style that is solely you.

- Don't be predictable. Mix and match pieces. Buying matching sets is not OK! What does work, however, is mixing various eras, styles, and collections. For instance, if you are drawn to glamorous pieces but teeter on the exotic, why not pair a mirrored nightstand with a zebra-print rug in the bedroom?

- Consider the architecture of the space, but don't be confined by it. Just because your home is midcentury modern doesn't mean you have to design it that way. However, you should stay true to some of the integrity of the home if it's in good shape. For instance, if you have gorgeous wood floors or intricate tile work, make it a focal point. Use these elements to help dictate the style of your home. And remember that paint and stain can change everything.

- Be confident. It's your home. Do what you love. After all, you're the one who has to live there!

DETERMINING YOUR BUDGET

- Budget is the most important factor in designing your space. You must be realistic and honest about what you have to spend. Like we did on *Design on a Dime*, you may find it helpful to write yourself a spreadsheet of everything that will go into the room, from the sofa to the paint. If you are hiring someone, don't forget to include labor costs, tools, and supplies. (Remember: you can't paint a room without a paintbrush.) It's important to stick to this list as diligently as possible. You'll be surprised how fast things add up. Nine times out of ten, the cost of a makeover is actually double what you think it will be.

- Always reuse and repurpose first, in order to save money for the pieces you really need. See what you already have and what needs to go. If a piece's structure is still in good shape, you may only need a fresh coat of paint. Remember that spray paint is a designer's best friend. If paint isn't enough and you still hate it, I give you permission to throw it away!

- Think multipurpose. When determining what you can spend on a piece, consider pieces that pull double duty. A dresser and a bed might not fit into your space or your budget, but a bed with built-in storage might.

- Mix it up and invest in high and low pieces. Pair an inexpensive sofa with expensive pillows, and it can instantly look like a million bucks. Give inexpensive chairs an upgrade with an expensive dining table. When working on a budget, consider the power of illusion. It works!

- Picking a color for your home isn't as easy as choosing just one color but rather selecting a combination of colors that work well together. To find your perfect paint palette, start by looking for inspiration. Turn to paintings, photographs, or even the colors in your wardrobe to find palettes that speak to you. This will give you a pretty good idea of what colors you gravitate towards.

DESIGNER TIP: Find a photo you like and use a color-matching tool to find out exactly what color combination is in that photo. It's priceless when picking colors for your home. Download an application on your phone or look online. My two favorites are the Behr ColorSmart Mobile App and Chip It!™ by Sherwin-Williams.

- Find one color that is your go-to color. For instance, my favorite color for my home is white. For me, white is calming. I never second-guess it. Once you decide what your go-to color is, you may want to incorporate it into every room. You'll be happy you did, and there will be an overall consistency in your home. Now, that's not saying you have to put the same blue pillows in every room of the house, but you can use blue pillows in the living room and then have a vase in the same gorgeous shade on the dining room table, and so on.

- Lighting changes everything. Chances are the paint color you choose won't look exactly the same on the wall as it does in the can. So before you commit, paint a piece of foam core first. Tape it to your wall and leave it up for several days. As the light changes in the room, so will the color. A great rule of thumb is to take into account which direction your room faces. An east-facing room will get more of the morning and evening sunlight, which means any shade of yellow or orange will get even warmer when the sun shines in, whereas the color in a north-facing room, with less direct light, will always stay relatively cool.

- Dark colors do—I repeat, do—work in a small space. You'd be amazed. Sometimes it even makes the room look bigger, by blurring the edges and making the space look like it goes on forever. Again, the trick is lighting. Every dark room needs appropriate lighting. In a room with no natural light, you must incorporate enough lighting around the space to keep the room from looking like a dark hole. I prefer dark colors for spaces that need a bit of drama, like powder rooms, hallways, and TV rooms. If you're apprehensive, paint one wall. You may find that one accent wall is enough.

- As a general rule, warm colors with hues of yellows, browns, and oranges can make the room feel a bit smaller than it is; cool colors like blues, grays, greens, and pinks can make the room look sparser. If you have a small space that looks as though it's closing in on you, opt for a cooler color. It may change the way you feel when you're in the space.

- Timeless color, such as black, white, navy, or brown, will never go out of style. For everything from your walls to your furniture, use textures and colors that have worked for generations. You can't go wrong with rich wood tones, classic paint colors, and timeless finishes.

- You might want to consider painting your walls last. I know this seems wacky, but it really does make sense. There are times when you will pick the perfect paint color but the rug, the sofa, and the table just won't make sense with it. Paint is probably the cheapest element to change in a room, so if you can, wait until you've picked your essentials before you pick your color. You'll be happy you did.

- When in serious doubt, consider the architecture of your home and do your research. This will give you an easy guide for what colors would look best within the structure of your home.

- To redesign a room, think beyond your walls to make a transformation. You can always add in color with your fabrics and accessories. A bold slipcovered sofa can look just as dramatic when pushed against a white wall.

FURNITURE AND SPACE PLANNING

- Think of every piece of furniture in your space as having a purpose. Does it operate as seating, storage, or dining, and is it the appropriate scale and shape? If you are still sitting on a futon in your living room, it may be time for a new sofa. Make note of what works and what doesn't. If it doesn't have a function, it doesn't belong. That's what accessories are for.

- Figure out how you use the space and what your overall ultimate vision is. Is it a place where the family cozies up to watch a movie or where you love to entertain? Design it with that in mind. A family space requires soft cozy furnishings, sofas to be sat on, and plenty of storage. Entertaining spaces need ample seating and inviting lighting. Make a list of the five most important things you'd like to incorporate in the space, and focus on those first.

- Measure and draw out your space. I can't stress this enough. There are numerous online space-planning tools available. Plug in the dimensions of your room and your furniture, and this will give you a good idea of how things will fit into your space. For example, you don't want to be stuck buying a sofa that won't fit through the front door!

- Use the space wisely, and make every room livable. Long gone are the days of the formal living room and dining room. Design to live in the room, and have fun.

- Mix up the size and scale of your furniture. Even small rooms need big pieces for balance. The height of the furniture also plays a big role in making the room seem proportioned. When in doubt, an eye-catching piece like a large-scale mirror or high chest of drawers can work in any space.

- Storage is a luxury! Smaller spaces can be charming and intimate. However, to avoid a cluttered appearance, invest in plenty of furniture pieces with hidden storage. A few great options are armoires that double as home offices, banquette seating with baskets or drawers underneath, or bookcases with pull-down tables. In addition, you can always increase the overall look of the space with large floor rugs, mirrors, reflective accessories, lighting, and glass.

- Never buy trendy furniture pieces. Invest in classic pieces that can be mixed with anything and that will look fantastic for the next twenty years. And if it's a family heirloom, cherish it, love it, and display it.

RECIPE FOR 5-MINUTE DECORATING

- Small bowls of candy, fruit, or fresh flowers add a punch of color.

- Lower the wattage of your lighting. Everything will look better.

- Switch out your sofa or bed pillows.

- Spray-paint a lamp base a different color and change out the shade.

- Replace your rug with a bright graphic print for a punch of color.

- Replace your throw on your sofa.

- Add a few interesting coffee table books.

RECIPE FOR DESIGNING LIKE A CELEBRITY

- If you can't afford the real thing, use faux expensive fabric. Velvet is always the best one to choose. It never fails to look rich and luxurious.

- Add thick countertops to your kitchen, and always get them in a honed (matte) finish.

- Dark-framed windows give a sense of mystery.

- Over-scale artwork makes a huge statement in any room.

- Designing for entertaining is a must. One of my favorite designers, Windsor Smith, creates kitchens that you don't just cook in but you entertain in. Consider creating a space where the dining room fits into the kitchen and isn't forced to hide in another room.

- Add ample bedding, or simply switch out those tired pillows with fluffy new ones.

- Hide your appliances. Create a kitchen that looks sleek and modern.

- Create a room with a view. The more you can see the beautifully manicured lawn, the better.

- Find an element that makes your space stand out. Install gorgeous molding on the walls, or add amazing wood floors. People will notice the details.

- Create an indoor/outdoor space. Even if you don't live in California, pretend you do. Instead of dining inside, bring the party to the yard, the deck, or even the balcony.

dining room

DINING ROOM

I recently read in a design magazine that you don't want the chandelier in your dining room to take the spotlight away from your fabulous food. Well, in this case I say let the chandeliers shine! This dining room makes my heart sing. I am in love! I believe in having a great entertaining space with interesting design elements, gorgeous lighting, and believe it or not, reading material. Whether you're having family dinners around a banquette or hosting a dinner party, inject character and charm into your dining room. Have fun with the space. After all, that's what it's meant for: friends, family, and food!

RECIPE FOR THE PERFECT DINING AREA

- If you love to entertain, it's important to add as much seating as your space will allow. Not having enough is always uncomfortable. Having extra foldout chairs is the perfect solution. Tuck them away, and pull them out when you need them.

- Matching dining sets are too predictable. Mix it up by incorporating different types of seating, such as benches, ottomans, upholstered chairs, or an array of chairs in the same style but different colors.

- Lighting is the most important element for creating your dream dining room. It can set the tone for the whole space. Most overhead lighting tends to be harsh. If your overhead doesn't cast a warm, welcoming glow, don't use it. Instead opt for floor lamps, table lamps that can sit on the credenza, or install dimmers, and always use additional candlelight for a dinner party. The room will have a nice glow, and everyone will look and feel more comfortable.

- Hang a chandelier roughly thirty-two to thirty-four inches above your tabletop. Its diameter should measure roughly 50 percent of your tabletop's surface. If your dining area is fairly large, you can always add more than one chandelier. Multiples are just as fun!

- When choosing a dining table, consider the adjoining rooms. If your dining space is connected to your living room, a round or oval table can break up the harsh lines of the sofa and coffee table. Likewise, mixing up materials, like putting a marble top on a wood base, can look classic and clean and less predictable.

- If you're putting a rug into your dining area, make sure the table and all the chairs fit comfortably on top of the rug. Choose a low-maintenance, low-pile or braided rug that won't snag on the chairs. Wool, nylon, or sisal work well.

- A bar cart in the dining room can act as a host when you're busy entertaining your guests or as storage if you are working with a smaller space. If you are in need of more storage than what a cart can hold, a credenza, console, or hutch is a great option. Keep your dishes, linens, and even board games in there when you're not using them.

- A dining room is a great place to experiment with molding, wallpaper, dramatic textiles, and paint colors. Have fun incorporating florals, stripes, geometric patterns, and bold colors. If you prefer a neutral and clean look, stick to colorful tablecloths that can be removed after dinner or as the seasons change.

- Mirrors and artwork will dress up any dining room and reflect the light. Install a mirror over your credenza or use a floor mirror to ultimately make the room look larger.

- Displaying a stack of books in your dining room is a must. Choose books that spark interesting dinner conversation. You'll be surprised at the discussion that books can elicit.

Iconic shapes and classic materials will never go out of style.

Go for a sculptural dining space with pieces that balance each other out. A pedestal table, sculptural chandelier, and curved chairs each hold their own weight without becoming overwhelming.

RUSTIC MODERN

I love the combination of simple, rustic, and modern pieces. Combining richly finished items with sculptural ones brings classic comfort to any dining space. This is something that Room and Board does so well. With edited-down pieces and mixed wood and steel, this room feels texturally simple but rich in design.

INGREDIENTS

Steel and Wood Parsons Dining Table
Black Lacquer Wood Chairs
Industrial Shelving
Wool Rug
Sculptural Pendant Lamps
Wood Planking for Wall

RECIPE

STEP 1: Install wood planks horizontally. This budget-friendly look brings texture and richness to a flat wall. Stain the walls the same color as the table to match the tone of the room.

STEP 2: Add a large wool rug in gray to keep a neutral base. Like the wood, wool is a natural and eco-friendly material that provides a softness to balance the wood and the steel.

STEP 3: Bring in a steel and wood dining table to combine the texture and matte look of the overall space. Its architectural, natural, and luxurious metal finish feels very current.

STEP 4: Surround the dining table with classic black lacquer chairs inspired by a 1953 Helge Sibast design. The simple bentwood chairs add an interesting shape next to a rectangular table.

STEP 5: For shelving and storage, go a little less conventional and use a bookcase. It's perfect for storing glassware, cookbooks, and textiles. Utilitarian in nature, steel and glass are simple and sophisticated.

STEP 6: Install multiple lighting sources at different heights. Stick with sculptural pieces that look handmade to bring home the Nordic look. The white pendants give a soft, quiet beauty to the room—exactly what you want in a dining space!

A bar cart is chic enough to hold all of your bar essentials without distracting from the overall design.

When picking artwork, choose pieces in the same medium and color for a unified look.

VINTAGE REVIVAL

A can of spray paint is every designer's best friend. Instead of leaving these vintage café chairs a cookie cutter color, Dayka Robinson painted them a sunny yellow, elevating this dining room to another level. This color accents the shape of the chairs and provides a cheery place to sit and enjoy your coffee in the morning.

INGREDIENTS

Neutral Wall Paint
Black Dining Table
Set of Matching Vintage Chairs
Ornate Mirror
Yellow Spray Paint

RECIPE

STEP 1: Sometimes less is truly more! For a clean and simple dining space with an open feel and high style, start with a subtle backdrop utilizing neutral wall colors and, if possible, natural wood flooring. No need for a rug—the goal is to let the furniture take center stage.

STEP 2: When furniture shopping, look for well-made pieces with lines and shapes that catch your eye and play well together. As with all secondhand furniture, make sure your pieces are in excellent structural condition and need little to no repair.

STEP 3: An eclectic mix of furniture works best when the lines in each piece either mimic each other or have a bit of contrast. However, you can never go wrong with pieces you truly love.

STEP 4: Select an oval or circular dining table, then look for chairs that mimic these same shapes—think Windsor or café chairs. The idea is to reinforce the overall shape of the table with the chairs.

STEP 5: Avoid the urge to be too matchy-matchy with your furniture. Determine the amount of seating you'll need, then select a set of matching chairs that work well with your table but aren't a part of the same dining room suite. Look for pieces with cool detailing or sleek modern curves, and mix it up.

STEP 6: Don't be afraid to go bold with color! In this case, the black table not only hides nicks and dents but also acts as a great neutral base for the bright yellow chairs. The key to pulling off this look is to have high contrast between the colors of the table and chairs. A black table is a great base to match with almost any color of chair, but don't shy away from white either! Whether your favorite style is country, modern, or traditional, be adventurous! Remember you can always paint any set of wood chairs you find.

continued

STEP 7: When selecting a wall mirror, the goal is to juxtapose the styles of the table and chairs. If your furniture is sleek and streamlined, look for a mirror with a lot of ornate detailing around the frame. If your table and chairs are detailed, choose a sleek and streamlined mirror to anchor your table in your space. Keep in mind that the size of your mirror will depend on the size of your dining room. Large room? Try using two to three smaller mirrors. Small room? Try one big mirror—the image reflection and sheer size will make it feel much bigger!

DAYKA'S DESIGNER TIPS: When in doubt, use high-gloss paint for added shine. Not only is it super durable, but glossy paint makes almost anything look good.

Keep in mind that when using mismatched dining chairs, it's very important to make sure the chairs are the same size and scale. Scale refers to dimension and proportion, and you want to ensure that the scale of each chair works well with the rest as well as with the table. You don't want to end up with one tiny chair and one huge chair and make a few of your guests feel like they belong at the kiddie table!

In a small banquette, midcentury pieces like these wishbone chairs work well. Their uncomplicated shape and appeal are simple yet sleek.

Live with your favorite pieces; don't tuck them away. Display family heirlooms and art together in the dining room to spark interesting dinner conversation.

A midcentury-modern credenza is great for style and storage.

LIGHT AND AIRY

Heather Scott's breakfast nook is a comfortable take on the traditional banquette. I love her use of soft upholstered chairs and a settee to create a peaceful retreat for the family to come together during the day. It's like bringing the living room to the dining room.

INGREDIENTS

One-by-Five-Inch Wall Boards (Shiplap)
White and Pale-Blue Paint
White Linen Fabric for Roman Shades
Sea Grass Rug
Round Glass-Top Table
Durable White Furnishings: Slipcovers and Teflon-Treated Materials

Punchy Pillows
Pair of Floor Lamps
Candleholder Chandelier

RECIPE

STEP 1: Transform a builder beige Sheetrock room into a cozy nook by applying tongue-and-groove shiplap wall paneling. Paint it bright white to make a small room feel larger, and paint the ceiling the palest blue to open it up and evoke the sky.

STEP 2: Purchase solid white linen fabric, cording, and wood board to make timeless Roman shades. It's quick and easy to do at home.

STEP 3: Add a simple sea grass rug to keep the room from looking too formal. All these elements create a white, bright, and neutral envelope to develop a coastal-inspired retreat in your home.

STEP 4: A round glass-top table is perfect for a small space. It keeps the room feeling open and gives you the flexibility to seat two to six people.

STEP 5: Mix up the seating by using a settee instead of traditional dining chairs to make the space more comfortable. In addition to being a place for family meals, this is now a great space for reading the paper and drinking coffee, working on your computer, or enjoying a glass of wine while chatting with friends. Durable velvet is used on the settee cushions, while the frame is covered in linen. Accent pillows add a punch of color to the room and can easily be changed seasonally or over time as your tastes change.

STEP 6: Add a pair of unique floor lamps to bring symmetry and balance to the room, making the setting pleasing to the eye. To save money on hiring an electrician, opt for a unique candleholder in place of a hand-wired chandelier.

HEATHER'S DESIGNER TIP: Make sure all the furniture materials are easy to care for by adding Teflon coating to the fabric before the furniture is made to protect it from spills or ink.

Go with a hutch for the biggest storage bang for your buck. Your decorative pieces can neatly be stored at the top while the bottom can hold your linens and bigger pieces.

Beautiful chandeliers are like the jewelry for your dining room.

Mod dining rooms are chock-full of classic furniture, retro wall art, and colorful pieces.

BOLD AND BEAUTIFUL

The dining room is one of the greatest places to play with wallpaper. The statement it makes is undeniable, so proceed with abandon. Go for the wow factor like Kati Curtis did by upping the ante with three designer pendants.

INGREDIENTS

Bold Patterned Wallpaper

Chair Rail

Antique Dining Table

Super-Modern Dining Chairs

Cushions

Antique Rug

Grayish-Blue Wall Paint

Large Round Pendant Lights

Art by Someone You Know and Love

Tea Set

RECIPE

STEP 1: Select a base color for your walls from one of the colors in your wallpaper. From the floor to thirty-six inches high, paint your wall color. Install the bold patterned wallpaper above the thirty-six inches. Once you've installed the wallpaper and painted the walls, you can install the trim pieces at thirty-six inches above the finished floor.

STEP 2: Have your electrician install modern pendants in a staggered pattern over where your table will go. A good rule of thumb is to have the pendants drop to thirty inches above the height of the table, but since you're staggering, make this the level of the lowest pendant.

STEP 3: Once the painting and any other finish work are complete, lay a rug pad on the floor centered under where your table will go. Throw the antique rug over the pad so it will stay put even when chairs are being pushed in and out from under the table. Make sure the rug is big enough to fit completely under your dining chairs so that you won't have wobbly seating.

STEP 4: Bring in the antique table, and center it under the pendants you've already hung. Place your modern dining chairs evenly around the table. If possible, you can have an upholsterer make cushions that fit inside your modern chairs.

STEP 5: Once your table and chairs are in place, hang a great piece of art created by someone you know and love. For a more unique and curated look, try not to match your artwork to the paper. Let it stand out all on its own.

STEP 6: Set the table with china, whether modern or your grandmother's. Again, mixing and matching styles is what it's all about.

STEP 7: Add fresh-cut flowers and macaroons, and you're ready for a proper tea.

DINING ROOM STARTERS AND SWEET TOUCHES

Make the back of your chairs as fabulous as the front.

For a rustic look, make a table out of old steel worktable legs and hang a rustic chandelier.

Let the ceiling shine with a DIY mirrored ceiling medallion. When the chandelier is on, the light will reflect off the mirrors, illuminating the entire space.

In a small kitchen, hang extra foldout chairs on the wall with a utility hook. They'll be ready for use when guests pop by.

RETRO GLAMOUR

When Kimberly Ayres was designing this dining room, her goal was to make it bright and fun. She scoured, shopped, and ultimately found the perfect place: eBay. Yes, this room came from eBay! A mix of eclectic and highly textured furniture pieces and bright colors turned this dining room into an online shopping success.

INGREDIENTS

Burl Wood Classic Parsons Table
Chippendale Chairs
Blue Faux Pigskin Fabric Buffet
Grass Cloth Wallpaper
Zebra Rug

Coral Chandelier
Wall of Mirrors
Photo/Painting Art

RECIPE

STEP 1: Start by picking your overall color scheme. The best way to do this is to let the color pick itself. Lay out your colors in the room and let them sit for several days. Depending on the light in the room, the colors will change and one will stand out. For this room, a bright yellow made the room feel happier.

STEP 2: Kimberly embraced the existing mirrored wall and added grass cloth wallpaper to give the room a bit of depth and to break away from paint. Go for a lighter color so the furniture stays the primary focus.

STEP 3: Add a designer table. A vintage Parsons-style burl wood table is a perfect choice for bringing in texture with a mix of yellows and browns.

STEP 4: Chippendale chairs, with their geometric backing, are vintage enough to carry on the theme. When coated with white lacquer and reupholstered in a bright yellow velvet fabric, they add a level of modernism.

STEP 5: Add a blue faux pigskin buffet for storage and to break up all the yellow pieces in the room. If you are undecided about faux pigskin, go for another texture like leather or suede. Just make sure it's a deep hue to tone down the yellow.

STEP 6: Create a focal point with art. While great art can always be bought online, ask around. Someone may know a great artist. This piece is a photo/painting combo done by two talented friends.

STEP 7: A sculptural chandelier in a coral motif adds to the whimsy feeling of the room and creates a gorgeous glow off the mirrored wall.

STEP 8: Finish up by adding a zebra-skin rug to break up the pale floors and to provide your final layer of texture.

Instead of covering a full wall, use strips of wallpaper and trim them out with molding.

These hand-embroidered coverlets, known as tenangos, are beautiful when draped across your table as a tablecloth.

Instead of adding artwork to dress up the walls, go for instant architecture by installing inexpensive picture molding painted stark white.

Pitchers rule, literally. Instead of the traditional vase, use something a little quirkier on the dining table.

For an eco-friendly look, choose pieces that are made from repurposed materials and buy locally. There are always artists in every area looking to sell their one-of-a-kind pieces.

CONVERSATIONAL DINING

Sally Wheat's dining room was designed to be a conversation piece. Packed with texture and finishes, this room is certainly a feast for your eyes. From the large-scale wallpaper to the curiosities placed around the room, there will be no lack of conversation here!

INGREDIENTS

Paisley Wallpaper
Sea Grass Rug
Plaster Chandelier
Wooden Table
Bench
Steel-Framed Vintage Chairs
Pair of Vintage French Campaign Chests

Lucite Bar Cart
Gilt Mirror
Sheer Linen Drapes

RECIPE

STEP 1: Select a large-scale patterned wallpaper in a muted neutral to give the room movement. This will provide enough visual interest without being too overwhelming.

STEP 2: Start by grounding the room with a large neutral sea grass rug.

STEP 3: Hang a big white chandelier above the dining table to illuminate the space. Incorporate round bulbs into the chandelier to give it more of a modern look.

STEP 4: Mix periods and styles! In order to create a room that is unique with tons of character, mix vintage, antique, and new pieces. Choose an earthy wooden table paired with modern, steel-framed vintage seats for an eclectic mix. Don't be afraid to mix and match seating. A furry, textured bench paired with four chairs is unexpected and fun.

STEP 5: Stack two vintage French campaign chests to act as a buffet. Top with a large antique gilt mirror.

STEP 6: Accessorize with interesting large conversation pieces, such as a bust. Decorate the bust with necklaces, hats, or flowers when entertaining to bring an interactive, playful element to the space.

MY DIY SLIDE PROJECTOR ART

We have what I like to call a slide show party at my house once or twice a year. That's where my photographer boyfriend plugs in his slide projector and we look at all the photos he's shot during the year on the wall of our living room. This year while looking at some of his photos, we came up with the idea to create artwork out of one of his photos. With an unused frame leaning against the wall, chalkboard paint, and a picture from a sunglasses case, a new art project was born.

INGREDIENTS

Old Large Frame
1 Cup of Black Latex Paint
2 Tablespoons of Unsanded Tile Grout
1 Piece of Hardboard Cut to Size
Chalk
Picture-Hanging Wire

TOOLS

Projector
Measuring Cup and Spoon
Paint Roller and Tray
Small Nails to Tack Wood to Frame
Hammer
Measuring Tape
Table Saw*

*Or have your local hardware store cut the hardboard for you.

RECIPE

STEP 1: Measure the interior of the frame. Have a piece of hardboard cut to sit inside the frame.

STEP 2: Thoroughly mix one cup of black latex paint and two tablespoons of unsanded tile grout. Paint the flat side of the hardboard.

STEP 3: When dry, nail the hardboard to the frame on the inside.

STEP 4: Using a projector, blast the desired image on the wall. Position the frame to sit exactly where the image is being projected.

STEP 5: Trace the image with chalk. Our image was a picture we took off of a sunglasses box. Use anything you'd like and have fun with it!

EMMA'S DIY WINDOW FILM

There are a few great ways to transform the look of your windows. One way is with window film. Years ago when I first discovered it, designs were pretty simple. Nowadays with designers like Emma Jeffs, they are more intricate and graphic. Use these anywhere around your home for privacy and to dress up your windows.

INGREDIENT

Window Film

TOOLS

Window Squeegee or Credit Card
Pencil
Spray Bottle
Cold Water
Tape Measure
Sharp Scissors
Window Scraper
Craft Knife or Razor Blade
Cloth

RECIPE

STEP 1: The night before application, unroll your film and place it fully open on a flat surface. Allow it to rest a minimum of eight hours to settle the natural curling and relax the tunneling (occasional separation of the film from the backing paper), making the application much easier.

STEP 2: Clean the glass thoroughly. Remove all paint spots with a window scraper. Let the area dry.

STEP 3: Measure the area to be covered. Measure in various places across and down to get the correct dimensions, as windows are not always straight.

STEP 4: Turning the film so the back faces you, measure out the dimensions of the surface and then add one-half inch of material on all sides. Cut using sharp scissors.

STEP 5: Lay the film with the pattern facedown on a tabletop. Gently peel off the backing paper. Be careful not to crease the film while removing the paper. Spray the film with a light coating of water as you peel the backing away. It's best to have one person spray as a second person peels the backing from the film.

STEP 6: Hold the top two corners of the film with your finger and thumb. Place the film on the glass and move it into position, lining up the top of the film with the top of the area being covered, and lightly press it into place.

continued

STEP 7: To carefully smooth out the film, place your squeegee or credit card at the top center of the film and make small sweeping movements outward toward each side of the film. Repeat this left-right motion moving down the length of the film, squeezing the water to the edges and bottom of the window. Stand back to check that all the bubbles have been removed. If not, go over the film again with the squeegee or credit card.

STEP 8: Trim the edges with a craft knife. Then smooth across the whole surface in all directions with a squeegee or credit card to help remove any remaining water or air bubbles.

STEP 9: If any bubbles still exist, pop the edge of the bubble with a pin and then squeeze the water toward the pinhole with your fingers.

STEP 10: The film now needs to dry for at least thirty-six hours. Any remaining condensation (foggy effect) between the film and window will dry during the course of the first week after the application.

DESIGNER TIP: Do not handle film when wearing clothes with loose fibers. Do not install in strong sunlight or on a very cold day. If covering an area more than thirty inches, it is easier to have two people handling the film. Clean only with a lint-free cloth, and do not use any abrasive materials or cloths. To remove, gently warm the surface with a hair dryer. Then peel back the film from one corner until you get a firm grip. When you are sure you have a firm hold, pull briskly away from the glass. Any remaining glue residue on the surface can be removed with mineral spirits and a window scraper.

Kitchen

KITCHEN

I once heard that people are judged on two areas of their home: their bathroom and their kitchen. With that said, I believe the kitchen is the heart of the home and should be given extra attention to be at its best. It's the room we gravitate toward and end up spending the most time in. Whether you're a gourmet chef or a killer peanut butter and jelly sandwich maker, having a great kitchen just makes everything taste better.

- Think about how you'd like your kitchen to function. What do you need most? Maybe it is storage, better lighting, or a paint refresher. Even on a budget, you can give your kitchen the face-lift it needs. Do your research and figure out what's realistic. Look through books and magazines and find styles and colors that speak to you.

- It's helpful to start with the cabinets because they are the biggest focal point in the room. A fresh coat of paint can do wonders! Going with a semigloss will work with any décor. However, if you're set on a modern lacquered finish, opt for a high gloss. In addition, consider painting the lower cabinets a different color than the top cabinets. This will intensify the overall look and anchor them. In consideration of your budget, opt for inexpensive cabinets and splurge on the countertop instead. No one but you will know the difference.

- If you are satisfied with the configuration of your cabinets but the outward appearance needs updating, opt for new fronts and then have the bases professionally sprayed. The coat will be even, and it will save you time and money in the long run. Other additions to consider are molding and glass. The molding will add a decorative element, while the glass will open up the space and make a small kitchen seem more spacious. If you're looking to really expand the space, remove the upper cabinets altogether and add open shelving. The look is marvelous, but you will need to be diligent to keep everything neat and clean.

- For a simple transformation, a fresh set of hardware on your cabinets can give them a refresher with the least effort. You can opt for knobs and pulls or add new hinges. Always bring the cabinet to the hardware store to ensure the proper fitting and save yourself from having to make a second trip.

- When it comes to changing out your countertops, you can choose from a variety of options, such as butcher block, marble, ceramic, stainless steel, manufactured stone, concrete, and laminate. With your budget and desired level of maintenance in mind, do your research and choose something with longevity. Not only do you want materials that will last, but you also want to pick a style that you will love ten years from now. Consider choosing a few different materials instead of just one, and mix and match. For instance, maybe you want a butcher block surface for your island and marble for your countertops.

- Appliances play a big role in the overall design of a kitchen. Stainless steel is a foolproof choice. If possible, choose energy-efficient appliances, which will help save you money over time. If your current appliances need a pick-me-up but you aren't able to invest in new ones, consider using appliance spray paint. For ten dollars, you can turn a dingy old refrigerator into one that looks brand-new.

- Simply updating your sink and faucet can make a big improvement in your kitchen. I always recommend letting the style of the kitchen dictate the style of your faucet and sink. If you are going for a more streamlined look, select a sink made of the same material as your countertop and go with chrome or brushed-nickel finishes. If you're looking for something a bit traditional, try a trough or stainless steel sink with a stainless faucet. Also take into consideration how you will use your sink. Do you own a lot of large pots and pans? If so, a single basin versus a double basin would be a better choice. For a more consistent look, choose a finish similar to that of your cabinet hardware. And always—and I mean always—splurge for a sprayer.

- Think of backsplashes as the backdrop of the kitchen. They're where you can inject color, pattern, and texture. Choose bead board for a rustic look, subway tile for a classic finish, glass tile for color, or even wallpaper covered with a piece of Plexiglas for a budget-friendly DIY option. With hundreds of options to choose from, this is where you can make a color statement in your kitchen. For an even bigger impact, extend the tile all the way to the ceiling.

- Floors ground the whole room, literally and figuratively. For instance, a really deep floor color can be a beautiful contrast to white cabinets, whereas concrete can make a home feel more modern. Before you purchase any flooring, think about its durability as well as its style/appearance. Not only do you want it to look good in your home, but you also want it to hold up to spills and foot traffic. Ceramic tiles are great for easy cleanup and come in a variety of textures and colors. Wood brings in warmth and coziness. There are also green options, such as eco-friendly cork, bamboo, or linoleum.

- Lighting can make or break a good kitchen design. Focus on task lighting and ambient lighting. It's always nice to incorporate some glamour or architectural detail, such as a lantern or a chandelier. For task lighting, think how you use the space and focus on lighting there. Under-cabinet lighting works well for cooking and prepping. It can also create depth in a small kitchen by allowing light to reflect off the backsplash. Your eye will focus around the room instead of in the center. And don't forget the dimmers. You'll need these to turn the lights up to cook and down to entertain.

- I love, love, love what I call stove-to-table kitchens, meaning you literally have your dining table in the kitchen and everything moves directly from the stove to the table. My favorite designer, Windsor Smith, accomplishes this with ease. The kitchens she designs are perfect for entertaining. She once told me that the best dinner conversations happen in the kitchen, so why not put the dining table there?

- If you don't have room for a dining table, maybe you can add an island with built-in storage. An island is a double-duty piece that gives prep chefs an added space to work on and guests a place to pull up a stool while you cook. For an inexpensive version, add some casters to a small cart and pull it out when needed.

Lucite shelving in a kitchen is a great modern alternative to wood shelving. It expands the space with its translucent effect and is more durable than glass.

Changing out your existing hardware for modern brass handles takes the cabinets from ordinary to extraordinary!

Don't be afraid to paint your floors. An amazing chevron pattern in the kitchen and dining room can give the floors a creative update.

WELL-BALANCED

It's all about balance, especially in Amber Lewis's kitchen. It's clean, textural, and industrial all at the same time! When your kitchen shares the same space as your living room, staying monochromatic offers an easy transition into the other spaces. To keep the overall design scheme of the big space consistent, Amber's philosophy is that every pristine piece in the kitchen should be paired with a textured element. This certainly created a sense of continuity with the living room. Obviously her philosophy works very well!

INGREDIENTS

Caesarstone Countertop
Marble Subway Tiles
Industrial Pendants
Classic Wall Sconce
White Shaker Cabinets
Vintage Kilim Rug
Industrial Chic Bar Stools
Greenery
Unfinished Wood Plant Containers
Chalkboard Paint on Pantry Doors
Nickel Hardware
Stainless Steel Appliances

RECIPE

STEP 1: You can't go wrong with white Shaker kitchen cabinets. Period. They possess character that works with the overall look of a kitchen. Not too modern yet not too ornate.

STEP 2: Make sure you install clean and crisp elements like white Caesarstone countertops. By picking a solid color, you can create a modern and sleek aesthetic.

STEP 3: A great backsplash is definitely worth splurging on. Amber used two-by-eight-inch Carrara marble subway tiles, which ultimately lend a modern shape to a classic material. Instead of stopping the backsplash at the upper cabinet level, take it all the way up the wall. By extending the marble up, it becomes much more of a visual feature and pumps up the overall look.

STEP 4: Add industrial lighting fixtures for an element of grit—literally! Amber used old hubcaps and got them wired for electricity, added an Edison bulb, and used a chain from the hardware store to suspend them from the ceiling.

STEP 5: Install a sconce over the sink. This sconce was once a task lamp from HomeGoods that was repurposed and mounted into the wall by simply taking off the bottom piece.

continued

STEP 6: Add seating. The stools tie in all the black accents with the rug and also ground the kitchen. Their industrial draft-like shape is another unexpected element that takes this kitchen from traditional to cool and eclectic.

STEP 7: Throw down a vintage Turkish kilim for age and warmth. It's also fantastic for adding color to the space.

STEP 8: Herbs planted in unfinished wood planters add a natural, rustic element. Remember: balance, balance, balance!

AMBER'S DESIGNER TIPS: For every clean, pristine item, add something contrasting. Pairing raw or unfinished wood with white glossy textures creates foolproof balance.

Kitchens should be as functional as they are beautiful, and you don't have to compromise one to get the other! Balance is the key with this kitchen. While clean and crisp, it's also cozy and inviting. This is achieved by adding elements that offset the white pristine factors that could otherwise lead to a completely sterile traditional kitchen.

In a small kitchen, forgo heavy cabinetry and make room for utility carts with rattan baskets for storage.

Go for a modern take on a very traditional style with an apron-front sink.

Sleek floor-to-ceiling white laminate cabinetry adds a modern touch to any kitchen. Pair it with a stainless steel backsplash to complete the look.

Stainless steel countertops, shelves, and appliances bring an industrial feel to a kitchen.

CLEAN AND CLASSIC

This is a perfect example of how to mix high- and low-end materials to make up a gorgeous and classic farmhouse kitchen. This airy palette can be achieved in any space and even on a smaller scale. But what truly got me was that the velvet bench and farmhouse-style table are in the kitchen rather than the dining room. I absolutely adore eat-in kitchens like Ingrid Oomen's. I love the option of entertaining your guests while cooking. Much less formal and so much more fun.

INGREDIENTS

Inexpensive Classic-Profile Cabinets
Crown Molding
Open Shelving
Stainless Steel Cabinetry
Favorite Warm White Paint
Industrial Lighting

Natural Marble Stone
Hardwood Floor
Large, Aged Table
Eclectic Seating
Inherited Dishes and Accessories

RECIPE

STEP 1: Choose factory-made cabinetry for the uppers. On a budget, inexpensive cabinetry is a perfect alternative to the more expensive versions and can look just as sleek when mixed with other high-quality materials, such as a marble backsplash and countertop. Be sure to choose a cabinet with a classic profile that is truly timeless. Warm white paint and crown molding give it a finished and higher-end look. For the additional cabinetry on the lower cabinets, go for stainless steel. The darker color grounds the space, and the material matches the other fixtures.

STEP 2: Select and install a natural stone countertop and backsplash in marble, which allows the space to feel natural while maintaining a clean and streamlined look.

STEP 3: Add traditional hardware and create open shelving that'll give you the added convenience of reaching everyday items.

STEP 4: Put in hardwood that has high contrast. Dark hardwood floors age with exquisite patina. With the contrast against the light walls, they create drama and will always look like they have aged with quality.

STEP 5: A large, well-loved table is prominent in any farmhouse. Its communal nature makes it a hub in the house and incredibly versatile. Add eclectic chairs for a touch of informality and charm. Try a velvet bench for some extra seating to infuse a sense of luxury. Who says you can't use velvet in the kitchen?

STEP 6: Add industrial lighting that alludes to the eclectic nature of a farm, where elements have been collected and repurposed over time.

STEP 7: To finish, incorporate a collection of inherited dishes, fresh flowers, or fruit. These elements add to the tactile nature of the space and can be changed up based on season and personal taste.

Storage is essential in a kitchen. Use bedroom closet doors to hide a pantry.

Vintage appliances bring in character. Have one re-chromed and it will look good as new.

Focus on the details. Rich textures and reflective pieces can make any kitchen stunning.

URBAN FARMHOUSE

Lyndsay and Fitzhugh from the Brooklyn Home Company pride themselves on designing homes they would want to live in. They love creating a hybridization of new and old to create timeless spaces. Their philosophy is that you should choose pieces you will never get tired of; this way you eliminate the need to redesign later. Several reclaimed pieces and a little bit of DIY have turned this kitchen into a space I like to call farmhouse chic.

INGREDIENTS

Farmhouse-Style 1930s Cast-Iron Sink
Gooseneck Faucet
Slate Countertops
Stainless Steel Appliances
Reclaimed Mahogany Island

Reclaimed Pine Shelving with Simple Brackets
Sink Skirt
Handmade Stools

*Dog not included

RECIPE

STEP 1: Start by choosing modern and vintage materials that will age well and look good in ten years. For the vintage pieces, choose ones that have character and will eventually develop a patina, such as reclaimed woods, old farmhouse elements, traditional fixtures, and timeless stone.

STEP 2: Go for the classics. True to the farmhouse design style, a classic 1930s cast-iron farmhouse-style sink offers a traditional touch to the kitchen. To eliminate the bulkiness of cabinets below and for a softer feel, incorporate a sink skirt to hide the legs and conceal storage. To finish the look, go for a traditional gooseneck faucet. The curve of the spout makes it look more vintage than modern.

STEP 3: Use a timeless material for countertops, such as slate. It has that modern English farm feel and will ultimately age with a gorgeous patina.

STEP 4: Mix and match countertop materials by using reclaimed mahogany wood as an island. For a handmade feel, pick up three pieces of reclaimed lumber and attach them using dowels and wood glue. Using a jigsaw, cut out the top to make a place for a knife butcher block, which can be attached underneath for easy access to your cutlery. Finish up by using a couple of coats of Danish oil to seal the piece, and attach it to a cabinet base.

STEP 5: Mixing modern and classic pieces is a way to ensure that the look always stays fresh. Go for modern stainless steel appliances even in a farmhouse kitchen to keep the look from going too country.

STEP 6: As an alternative to upper cabinetry, attach reclaimed wood pine shelves with simple brackets for storage. Adorn with copper, stainless, and white china for a cleaner look.

STEP 7: Scour wood mills for stumps that can be transformed into rustic stools for extra seating around the island.

Use an outdoor table indoors. A repurposed zinc tabletop placed on an industrial base makes a great conversation piece.

Skip traditional luminaries in a kitchen and use something a little more alluring, such as a chandelier.

Choose a large floor rug in a kitchen with an open plan to make the room appear bigger.

POOL HOUSE

Muse Interiors' design objective for this pool house was to create a serene area where adults could entertain at night and a young family could relax during the day. They wanted a chic, modern look that was just as functional as it was beautiful. Although they were working in a space with very high ceilings, the footprint itself was small. Careful plotting and planning with Lucite, mirrors, geometric patterns, and marble turned it into an oasis.

INGREDIENTS

Globe Pendant
Hardwood Flooring
Lucite Stools
Honed Calcutta Marble Countertop
Grayish-Blue Wall Paint
Gray Floor Paint
White Mirror
White Shelving
Roman Shade
Sea Glass Accessories

RECIPE

STEP 1: Start with your paint. In this case, the wall and floor colors were pulled from the fabric used for the window treatment. Just like art, your fabric can dictate the colors to use in your space.

STEP 2: Make a custom island base and top it off with salvaged wood and a marble countertop to make things seem old and weathered yet warm and modern.

STEP 3: To keep a casual beach house aesthetic to the kitchen, install a ceruse oak wood floor and carefully plan out and paint a checkerboard pattern over the top using gray paint. The geometric pattern will liven up the space and also make it seem larger than it is. If you have an existing wood floor, you can always pickle or whitewash it to get the same effect.

STEP 4: Install a globe pendant to help balance the height of the room and give the room added light.

STEP 5: Add a mix of easy-to-maintain surfaces and accessories, such as Lucite stools, white shelving, sea glass vases, and a big wall mirror to reflect the suspended light.

STEP 6: Hang the custom Roman shade to dress up the window and tie all the colors of the room together.

A painted Union Jack backsplash is an entertaining backdrop for a kitchen.

A chalkboard backsplash is an inexpensive alternative to tile.

A galley kitchen gets a touch of glamour with a beautiful chandelier and supersized artwork.

A metal utility cart does double duty in a kitchen, offering surface space and storage.

Give your guests a place to sit by incorporating a sofa into your kitchen space.

HOMEMADE

Jenifer Porter, owner of Chic Living LA, has everyone's dream kitchen—a large space that makes use of every square foot. It's a perfect place for a family to gather, for a cook to create, and for friends to converse. Big on comfort, style, and sophistication, this kitchen is a livable space for every family member and guest!

INGREDIENTS

Dark-Stained Prefinished Oak Floors
White Carrara Marble Countertops
Gray-Green Subway Tile
White Raised-Panel Custom Cabinetry
Gray Caeserstone Island Countertop
Tufted Custom Banquette in Commercial-Grade Faux Leather
Upholstered Banquette Chairs
Custom Oval Dining Table
Stainless Steel Appliances and Fixtures
Chrome Light Fixtures
Gray-Green Wall Paint
Chrome Chandelier
Chandelier
Belgian Linen Roman Shades in Greige

RECIPE

STEP 1: Using a classic paint palette, cover the walls in a gray-green paint. This classic hue adds warmth and depth to the walls and works well with all the elements in the space.

STEP 2: You can never go wrong with classic white, raised-panel cabinetry. Traditionally designed, these cabinets offer a sense of formality with simple lines and stately legs. Instead of raising the cabinetry to the ceiling, opt for glass doors that lace the top of the cabinets for an open, airy feel and plenty of storage. Stainless knobs continue the classic look.

STEP 3: Countertop space is essential. A thick slab of Carrara marble suits the large space. It's sophisticated, and the veining in the marble gives a textural feel to the surface. Install the Carrara countertop on the perimeter of the space, opting for a gray Caeserstone on the island to mix up the look.

STEP 4: Instead of the typical white subway tile, install green glass subway tiles with a glossy finish to dress up the backsplash. The style is classic, yet the color is refreshingly new.

continued

STEP 5: Industrial-strength classic appliances should grace any cook's kitchen. Stainless steel reflects the light in the space and will always look great.

STEP 6: Different areas need different lighting sources. A chandelier over the island and seating area is perfect for both task lighting and mood lighting. Mixing and matching the styles keeps the look utilitarian and classic.

STEP 7: Extra seating is always important in a big kitchen. A tufted custom banquette in faux commercial-grade leather is the perfect nook. In addition, two upholstered chairs provide extra seating around a custom table, allowing your guests to be part of the action and adding a level of comfort to the space.

STEP 8: Prefinished oak wood flooring in a dark stain grounds the room with richness. Its heavy, open-grained look is masculine and ideal in any traditional kitchen.

STEP 9: Last but not least, soften the look of the windows with Roman shades made from Belgian linen in greige. The soft folds and light texture give the room privacy without sacrificing sophistication.

For a whimsical touch, use classic jars with chalkboard stickers to identify the contents.

Playful artwork bought on Etsy can dress up any kitchen. Just stick it up with industrial-strength Velcro so you don'tdamage any walls or tiles.

BEACH GALLEY

When you rent a place, there is only so much you can do to transform the space without feeling like you're putting all your money into someone else's pocket. Case in point: my kitchen. This small galley kitchen in an otherwise large beach apartment definitely needed a bit of DIY. With limited time and money, the essentials were changed out and my rental kitchen was turned into a permanent beauty.

INGREDIENTS

White Paint
Statuary Marble Subway Tile
Black Modular Granite Countertop
Pendant Light Fixture
Koa Wood Flooring Planks
Stainless Steel Gooseneck Faucet
Stainless Steel Sink
Brushed Nickel Knobs

RECIPE

STEP 1: Galley kitchens tend to be quite small. Going monochromatic with your color scheme can make the room seem a bit bigger than it is. Start by painting the walls and cabinetry the same color to give a nice flow to the kitchen and create a sense of continuity. White works well in such a small space, making it feel light and airy.

STEP 2: Create the illusion of more surface space where there isn't any. Just like black on any other surface, opting for a countertop in a deep, dark color will make the countertop look as though it's larger. Choosing a modular one like this is perfect for people who would like to do it themselves. Cheaper than a full slab, it comes in pieces that can be set into place without the expensive price tag or the heavy installation.

STEP 3: Install a backsplash to tie the whole look together. This is the best place to incorporate color and pattern and can set the tone for the whole kitchen. Going with a statuary marble keeps the look classic and versatile. Again, going with subway tile versus a full slab will save you money and be easier to install.

STEP 4: Go for texture. One way to incorporate texture into your space is with your flooring. Snap individual wood planks into place. Using Koa wood or any wood with a lot of texture warms up the space.

STEP 5: Match your sink, faucet, refrigerator, and knobs for a clean look. Going with stainless steel makes the whole kitchen feel more modern.

STEP 6: Add a hanging pendant with an exposed bulb to keep the light clean and bright.

Wooden cutting boards artfully displayed on the kitchen wall are functional and decorative.

Add more flavor to your kitchen by placing a table lamp on your countertops. Perfect for extra task lighting.

Inexpensive jars are a great place to store your baking ingredients. Handmade labels like Kristine Franklin's make baking a little more fun and also double as cute countertop décor.

INGREDIENTS

Image to Transfer
Clear Decal Paper (blue watermark on back)
Magic Paper (attached translucent protective paper)
Water
Soft Cloth
Glass Jars

TOOLS

Ink-jet Printer
Laminator
Scissors
Microwave, Oven, or Hair Dryer

RECIPE

STEP 1: Decal paper comes in clear or white. Be sure to buy the clear paper, which provides a transparent background around the image. Print your image onto the glossy side of your decal paper using an ink-jet printer. Do not mirror your image. After printing, allow it to dry thoroughly.

STEP 2: Separate the translucent protective paper from the magic paper. Do not throw the translucent paper away.

STEP 3: Place the magic paper gloss-side-up on your table. Lay the decal paper printed-side-down on top of the magic paper. Place the translucent protective paper gloss-side-down on top of the decal paper. Some images take up the entire sheet of decal paper so you do not need to trim around those first. If you are working with a smaller image, you may wish to cut roughly around it with scissors.

STEP 4: A basic laminator can be bought for about twenty dollars at most office supply and department stores. Laminate your stack of three papers together on low speed and at low temperature.

STEP 5: Discard the translucent paper. Your decal paper and magic paper should now be fused. Trim closely around your image. You can see it quite easily through the paper if you hold it up to the light. Where there is no ink, the decal will leave a very fine, slightly translucent film, which is visible close up or at certain angles. If your image is text alone with no border, the neatest finish is a nice even box. (Trying to mimic the outline of the text can look messy.) If your image has a distinct border, then trim approximately two millimeters all the way around it. Leaving a small buffer ensures you get a good seal.

STEP 6: Dampen the back (the watermarked side) of the decal paper with a cloth until it becomes translucent. Wait about fifteen seconds, then gently peel the paper away completely. It is important that you remove the watermarked decal paper only at this stage.

continued

STEP 7: Quickly immerse the decal in a shallow dish of water to dampen the other side. Then position it image-side-down on your jar, smoothing it down with your fingers and a slightly damp cloth to remove excess water.

STEP 8: Carefully slide off the backing paper and manipulate the decal into its exact position. Continue to smooth it until it is free of water and air bubbles.

STEP 9: Finally, set the decal using one of the following methods:
- Baking in an electric oven for eight minutes at 150 degrees Celsius.
- Cooking in a microwave for five minutes on low.
- Blowing with a hair dryer for five to ten minutes.

MICHAEL'S DIY PEG-BOARD

Storage can be tricky in a small space. Try using a twenty-dollar Peg-Board to hang your kitchen essentials. This is a simple DIY project that's extremely functional.

INGREDIENTS

Peg-Board
White Paint
Utility Hooks
Metal Wire

TOOLS

Paint Roller
Table Saw or Circular Saw
Measuring Tape
Pencil

RECIPE

STEP 1: Start by measuring out and marking the desired length and width of the Peg-Board.

STEP 2: Using your circular saw or table saw, cut the piece to length.

STEP 3: Give your Peg-Board a coat of white paint. Repeat if necessary. Let dry.

STEP 4: Install utility hooks and wires by slipping them into the holes.

STEP 5: Hang pots, pans, and kitchen essentials.

SIBYLLE'S DIY KITCHEN CART

Sometimes just a little added surface space can help. Transform a bar cart into storage that can be wheeled around a small kitchen.

INGREDIENTS

Kitchen Cart
Wall Bottle Opener
Various Hooks
Black Paint for Lettering
Stencils
White Paint
Set of Casters

TOOLS

Measuring Tape
Circular Saw
Drill
Paintbrush
Pencil

RECIPE

STEP 1: Start by measuring the height of the casters. Measure the same length on two of the bar cart legs. Using your circular saw, cut off the ends of the two legs where you've marked them.

STEP 2: Using your drill, screw on the casters.

STEP 3: Give the bar cart a coat of white paint. Repeat if necessary, allowing time to dry.

STEP 4: Stencil *EAT* on the cart and fill it in with black paint.

STEP 5: Attach a bottle opener and any added hooks.

BRIAN'S DIY PHOTO BACKSPLASH

Who needs hanging art for the kitchen when you can line the walls with it? Personalize your kitchen with a photo backsplash. Cheaper than tile and a fun conversation piece for sure!

INGREDIENTS

Favorite Photograph
Gallon of Wall-Covering Primer
Wallpaper Paste
Roll of Contractor Paper
Long, Flat Prep Surface
Dishwashing Soap
Hot Water
Painter's Tape

TOOLS

Spackle
Putty Knife
Sanding Block
Wallpaper Smoothing Tool
High-Resolution Scanner
Local Digital Printer
Tape Measure
Paint Pan and Liner
Bucket
Sponge
Level
Drop Cloth
Pencil
Paint Roller

RECIPE

STEP 1: Choose the proper image. Edit your photo collection down to subjects with clean, graphic lines with complementary shape, scale, and proportion to the backsplash. Once an image is selected, determine if it is high resolution or low resolution. If the image is low resolution, request a high-resolution scan at a local photo-processing lab. Next, contact a local digital printer and have the image printed onto laminated UV-resistant vinyl based on the dimensions of the backsplash wall.

STEP 2: Make a template. Unroll the contractor paper, cut it to the width and length of the backsplash wall, adding a few inches on either side. Tape the paper to the wall, trace the parameters of the cabinets and countertops to the paper, and cut it to size with a utility knife. Remove the paper from the wall and roll up the template.

STEP 3: Prep the backsplash area. Protect your countertops and kitchen floor with a drop cloth. Use a putty knife to fill holes or dents in the wall with spackle. Allow time to dry, then sand it smooth with a sanding block. Wipe dust from the wall with a damp sponge that's been dipped in hot, soapy water. Pour wall-covering primer into the paint pan liner, and using a paint roller, cover the backsplash area with a coat of wall-covering primer.

continued

STEP 4: Lay the vinyl out on a long, flat surface with the printed image facedown. Place the template on top of the vinyl, trace lines with pencil. Use the utility knife to cut the vinyl along the penciled line.

STEP 5: Adhere the photo backsplash. Perform a dry fit by placing the vinyl against the wall, ensuring the correct size and shape. Remove the vinyl and pour wallpaper paste into the paint pan liner. Using another paint roller, apply paste to the wall. After five to ten minutes, press the vinyl against the wall, smooth out air bubbles with a smoothing tool, and cut away the excess vinyl with the utility knife.

STEP 6: Fill a bucket with hot, soapy water. Dip a sponge in the bucket, then fully wipe all the wallpaper paste residue from the front of the vinyl. Repeat three or four times until the surface is clean.

KRISTIN'S DIY BRASS BOWL KITCHEN LIGHT

Flea markets are the best places to pick up inexpensive items to repurpose. Kristin picked up this brass bowl and reconfigured it to be a kitchen light. The reflective nature of the brass made it perfect for shedding a little light on her kitchen and adding a bit of glam.

INGREDIENTS

Flea Market Brass Bowl
Standard Household Light Kit
Lightbulb

TOOLS

Metal Hole Saw
Drill
Tape Measure
Marker

RECIPE

STEP 1: Measure the exact center of the base so the light sits evenly after it's installed.

STEP 2: Drill a hole in the base the size of the light socket at the center point.

STEP 3: Put together the light kit. Insert the socket into the base and the bulb through the opposite end to secure.

STEP 4: Secure the light kit to the ceiling with a ceiling mount or hook.

STEP 5: Plug in the light kit or hire your favorite electrician!

kids room

KID'S ROOM

What I love about a kid's room is that anything goes. It's the chance for adults to be kids again and have fun with the décor. While I'm not big on themed rooms, per se, there are a lot of options for designing a child's space without going overboard. Whether you prefer the clean lines of modern furniture, the charming nature of vintage décor, or the vibrant colors and patterns in mixing eclectic pieces, it certainly can be done in such a way that it's appealing to you and your child. Ultimately, the priority here is that the space is functional, safe, visually stimulating, and comfortable. You want it to be a place where your child can be adventurous, learn, and grow.

RECIPE FOR A KID'S ROOM

- Walls in a kid's room can be a fun place to experiment with color. If you plan to paint, it's always smart to go with a non-VOC paint. It emits fewer toxins, which is healthier for everybody. To select a color for your space, find a pattern you like as inspiration. Pull all the colors from it, and use them around the room. It'll be the easiest way to make sure every color in the room stays consistent.

- If your child's room will eventually be converted into another space, you can always stick with a neutral color. Other options are incorporating stripes, classic wallpaper like grass cloth, or decals so it can easily be transformed later. Remember you don't have to sacrifice color and style. Just keep the overall colors timeless and it will work for every transition.

- Don't forget the ceiling. Think of how cool it would be to look up to stripes or the blue sky every morning. Make things visually interesting for your child by painting the ceiling a fun color and/or pattern. You may even want to wallpaper the ceiling.

- Kids' rooms can be expensive, so it's imperative to design smart. Opt for furniture that kids can grow with. There is no rule that says you have to use kids' furniture in the room. Family heirlooms, midcentury-modern furniture, storage lockers: these are all great choices. Repurposing items is always a great idea too. Hand-me-downs take on a whole new life when given a fresh coat of paint. One big thing to keep in mind when choosing these pieces is safety. Although it may look good, if you're hesitant about the safety of the structure, don't use it. Make sure it's void of any lead paint, sharp corners, loose pieces, or missing parts. And be sure to tether freestanding furniture, such as a dresser, to a stud in the wall to avoid tipping.

- Storage is key here. Some solutions are ample plastic bins, baskets, ottomans with hidden storage, beds with built-in storage, lockers, shelving, desks with built-in storage, and bookcases. One of my favorite storage components is an old television armoire. I love it because it can play double duty. You can give it a good sanding and repaint it with chalkboard paint. (You can make your own any color by using unsanded tile grout and latex paint.) Now the kids have not only a place to store their things but also an art station.

- Fabrics in a child's room give the room life and texture. I like to always go for sheets and fabrics that feel good to the touch. I want them to be comfortable and cozy. I like to think of how I would want it to feel and go from there. Of course, durable fabrics that are washable are the best choices here.

- Another fabric to consider is your window treatments. Dress up the windows with drapes, Roman shades, or both to create layers. For added detail, hang them or embellish them with items like rope rings or ribbon. Also opt for blackout drapes or shades to minimize the light that comes into a baby's room to encourage naps.

- Play up the lighting. Kids need ample lighting to read and play, so the light should be brighter here. Traditionally, wall sconces can be a great option for task lighting or reading by the bed, but an overhead works better for the general function of the space. Try to avoid the standard flush-mount lights, as I tend to find the lighting can be quite unpleasant and harsh. Instead, go for a chandelier, a funky light fixture, or a modern hanging pendant. The room will look more styled and designed and less like you bought everything at your local hardware store.

- Chances are your child will be playing on the floor, so it's important to keep flooring in mind. A durable, easy-to-clean, nonslip option should be first and foremost. Always add a rug to provide a place for your child to hang out. This will give you a chance to incorporate color, pattern, and texture into the space as well. Choose rugs with natural fibers, such as cotton, wool, and silk.

- Finally, accessorize with your child's art. Frame his or her drawings, paintings, and photos for a more personalized space. Have a craft hour when your child can be an imaginative little Picasso. Your child will feel proud and take ownership for designing the space.

FRESH AND PLAYFUL

This room's palette consists of two main colors: orange and aqua. Keeping everything simple and neutral, Anyon Interior Design created layers with stripes, fun patterns, and subtle pops of color. With a great overall foundation, the transition from baby to toddler will be easy.

INGREDIENTS

One Graphic Print Fabric in Bright Colors
Crib Bedding That Coordinates
Horizontal-Striped Walls
White Lacquer Furniture
Side Table with Pop of Color

Soft Neutral Sea Grass Rug
Vintage and New Books and Toys
Photography and Art

RECIPE

STEP 1: Pick two favorite accent colors to inspire your palette. Orange and aqua were used here, which could easily be changed to raspberry pink and aqua for a more feminine room.

STEP 2: Hunt for a graphic print fabric that incorporates your accent colors. Use this fabric to make draperies or Roman shades. Make sure to line them with blackout liner so baby can nap during light hours.

STEP 3: Paint the walls in subtle neutral stripes to add a playful dimension to the room. Use a kid-friendly, eco-friendly paint.

STEP 4: Add a soft neutral rug. Invest in one that you will want to keep for years and that your baby can eventually roll around on.

STEP 5: Ground all the color you've added by using white or neutral furnishings. This includes your bookcase, crib, and changing table. You can always have fun mixing white and wood. Ultimately, the monochromatic palette will unify them.

STEP 6: Add a comfortable glider chair for rocking baby to sleep. Upholster it in a soft white outdoor fabric, which can easily be spot cleaned.

STEP 7: Find one small piece of furniture, such as the side table shown, with a pop of color. Here a vintage rattan table was lacquered to match the orange in the palette.

Kitchen cabinets in a kid's room are a great resource for storage!

Midcentury-modern pieces are perfect for a kid's room. They are classic in design, and a child can grow with them.

Create a nursery mobile using a branch from the backyard and some handmade paper cutouts. It's budget friendly and fun to make.

Modern and cool, a suspended clear acrylic bubble chair turns a kid's room into a teenage playground.

Horizontal wood planks and a handmade linen headboard turn this room into a cozy retreat!

Create a little nook with fabric. It's perfect for curling up and reading a book or taking a nap in.

LOVE

COLOR AND CONTRAST

Rachel Oliver knows how to use different shades of the same color to create depth. The corals and reds blend with blue, white, and black in striking detail. What caught my eye, however, were these wallpaper headboards, which are great for dressing up a space with just a few materials. A few simple DIY projects later, and we have a room packed full of color and pattern!

INGREDIENTS

Graphic Wallpaper with Large Organic or Figurative Pattern
Geometric-Patterned Fabric
Brightly Painted Round Mirror
Wall-Mounted, Curvy Nightstand
Decorative Molding
Bold, Striped Throw Pillows Decorated with Ribbons

Plush Oriental Rug
Bedspread and Quilt
Sconces with Shades
Half-Inch Grosgrain Ribbon
Shadow Frames
Seashells

RECIPE

STEP 1: Pick three colors that complement each other. In this room, coral, sea blue, and dark gray made a perfect palette. A lighter shade of paint applied to the wall keeps the room nice and bright. The key to this look is to pick your colors and stick with them. You can use different shades of the same color. By keeping a nice balance of contrast, pattern, texture, and color, you are well on your way to a fun, fresh room!

STEP 2: Create the illusion of a bigger headboard with wallpaper. The wallpaper should be high contrast with a large pattern. If you don't want to do any construction with the molding, use a wide two-inch ribbon and apply the same way as described in step 5 for the faux crown molding.

STEP 3: Incorporate furniture. Be sure the headboards are low enough to show off that fabulous wallpaper. To save some money, you can skip the headboards altogether and bring the wallpaper panels lower and use them for the headboard.

STEP 4: To mimic a very expensive fabric, these throw pillows were made by sewing lengths of ribbon onto a flat piece of linen and using that as the front of the pillow. Use a darker contrasting color for the ribbon.

STEP 5: Ribbon can also be applied to the bottom of the crown molding or where the ceiling meets the wall for a simple faux crown molding. Dip ribbon into liquid starch and apply to the wall while wet. Clean up drips with a sponge.

STEP 6: Paint the mirror and shadow boxes the same color, and secure interesting seashells into each shadow box with hot glue. Hang with pretty cording from picture molding hooks so you don't have nail holes in the wallpaper.

STEP 7: Add a traditional rug to break up the carpeting and add some color and texture to the floor.

Two stark-white matching headboards in an interesting yet similar shape give this room a bit more character.

A gorgeous vintage bed brings a little bit of glamour to a teen's room!

The smallest wall sconce can act as ample reading light above the bed.

In a kid's room, use classic fabrics to punch up the preppy!

OUT OF THIS WORLD

Turning stripes from vertical to horizontal transforms a boy's room from traditional to modern. Freed from the constraints of a typical boy's bedroom design, Martha Angus doesn't just see things in black and white but infuses bold pops of color with a futuristic feel.

INGREDIENTS

Striped Wallpaper
Jute Area Rug
Grass Weave Roman Shades
Parsons Desk
Art
Swivel Desk Chair
Groovy Lounge Chair
Orange Floor Lamp
Desk Lamp
Accessories

RECIPE

STEP 1: Think outside the box and turn typical vertical-striped wallpaper horizontally. This will make the room appear larger and draw your eye around the space.

STEP 2: Select neutral window and floor coverings to create the perfect foundation for the many items associated with a spirited kid's room. These add a level of sophistication.

STEP 3: Mix simply designed pieces, such as an inexpensive Parsons desk, with a fun, modern desk chair. Again, they're grounded in simplicity and yet teeming with significance for your important little person.

STEP 4: Select an exciting, artful lounge chair that is functional, interesting, and captures the imagination of your young one for the extraordinary things in life.

STEP 5: Continue the marvel and wonder of intriguing shapes and colors with a retro floor lamp in bright orange with a bell-shaped shade. Include a few other corresponding bright orange accessories to permeate the space with pops of color.

STEP 6: For the final and most important touch, include noteworthy art. Children appreciate it as much as adults do! It can be sculptural or framed art on the wall. Roy Lichtenstein is an especially graphic, lively, and noteworthy option for any room but particularly for the imaginative child in your home.

Create high style with a custom canopy. It's sophisticated and feminine.

Small lockers on wheels can serve as nightstands and storage.

To make a communal space more comfortable, keep the décor streamlined and give everyone a sconce for reading.

Be dramatic with patterns. Covering everything with the same fabric creates a fun fantasy room.

BEACH BUNGALOW

Inspired by the house's architecture, this gorgeous beach home from Rethink Design Studios, with its crisp white palette and bold pops of color, is meant to hold an entire family for weeks at a time. Matching beds do double duty with ample storage underneath. Replacing typical curtain rings with rope gives this home a perfect beach feel. My favorite part, though, are the headboards that resemble the seat cushions in my grandpa's boat. Priceless.

INGREDIENTS

Built-in Storage
Marine Reading Lights
Yellow Box Cushions with Handles
White Privacy Curtains
Nautical Rope
Painted Floorboards
Vintage Nightstand
Black-and-White Rug
White Bedding
Rickrack Lampshade
Personal Accessories and Memorabilia

RECIPE

STEP 1: Start by letting natural daylight flood the space by painting the walls and floors white. Architectural details like casement windows and wood panel ceilings give enough visual interest and depth to keep the all-white living area from looking flat and washed out. Spend your money on architecture instead of filler. A room with enough architectural interest doesn't require as much furniture to look finished.

STEP 2: Make your space do double duty. Maximize the amount of sleeping space by aligning built-in twin beds on either side of the stairs with ample storage underneath. For headboards, hang box cushions with handles above the bed that also serve as additional floor seating for an informal game night on a rainy day.

STEP 3: Place personal niches on either side of the beds to provide additional storage and allow guests to customize their spaces. Just because you're at the beach doesn't mean you need to sacrifice technological amenities. Be sure to include hidden outlets to keep the space functional and desirable for all ages.

STEP 4: Add a graphic black-and-white rug for a bit of texture and color. For a vintage touch, add a nightstand and lamp between the beds. To give the room a bit more light, install a marine reading light above each of the beds.

continued

STEP 5: To give ample privacy to the bedrooms without sacrificing the light and airy feel (or your budget), use white linen curtains hand-strung with nautical rope. When not in use, the curtains can be drawn back to create a loft-like living area. This incorporates a nautical element and a custom look for less. Simply buy standard-sized drapes and use the rope to make up the difference.

STEP 6: To create additional architectural character and nautical style, integrate driftwood-colored beams and headers. Not only do these visually break up the white space; they add age and warmth by merging the textures of sea and shore. Go to your local lumberyard and ask to see any large beams or boards that have been left out in the sun. The sun will gray out the natural wood and leave you with a house that blends contemporary ideas with old nautical charm.

STEP 7: Avoid the beach house stereotype by moving away from the traditional marine imagery of boats and shades of navy. The collage wall maintains its cohesiveness with similar neutral tones and the use of the nautical rope in a new and creative way. Include personal family photos and works of art with punches of yellow to bring a fresh feel of summer. When creating a collage wall, remember that repetition is key and no single element should draw too much attention. If you want to add a bright color, make sure to distribute it in multiple areas.

RETHINK DESIGN STUDIOS' DESIGNER TIP: Marry old pieces with new. Here, several pieces were owned by the family previously and given new life through the use of powder-coating and fresh paint. This allows any items the family holds dear to work with the new design yet maintains sentimental value.

Go retro in a beach house with a surfer-chic theme complete with a porthole!

Eye-catching design in a kid's room starts with bold colors and patterns. Pick two bright colors and one neutral, and go for it!

An under-the-bed cubby can turn into a think tank for the little ones!

Naomi Mann wanted to create a sustainable nursery that was a place for a child's imagination to soar. The client's wish was to have a space that could easily be converted into a nursery for more children and then one day into an office. This room is a true representation of being sustainable with its new items, old items, locally made furniture, and organic fabrics with eco-friendly dyes.

INGREDIENTS

White Wall Paint
Sustainable Furniture
Natural Fiber Rug
Custom-Made Chair and Ottoman
Organic Light Fixture
Family Heirloom Wall Mirror
Organic Window Treatment
Accessories Made by Local Artisans

RECIPE

STEP 1: For a room to be easily transformed in the future, start by painting the walls with a non-VOC white paint. This will serve as a good foundation.

STEP 2: Choose a natural fiber rug free of any synthetics, which can easily work in a nursery as well as an office.

STEP 3: Incorporate sustainable furniture that has a modern feel. A white crib, dresser, and changing table are the perfect staples for any nursery. Incorporating interchangeable pieces and double-duty furniture is a great way to save money later.

STEP 4: Purchase organic fabric by the yard for all your fabric pieces. Have an upholsterer make a custom chair and custom window shades using only natural organic fabrics.

STEP 5: Use any leftover fabric and have a custom drum shade made for your ceiling fixture.

STEP 6: Incorporate a few natural elements for an organic feel. These wood shelves are reclaimed wood treated with a nontoxic sealant.

STEP 7: Purchase accessories from local artisans who have products made from recycled and sustainable materials. In this case, the mobile was made from recycled cards.

NAOMI'S DESIGNER TIP: When creating a room that will eventually be transformed into a few other spaces, consider furniture pieces that will be the constant building blocks. In the end, it will look good in every design.

An adorable decal like this one takes the cute factor up a few notches.

Painting light horizontal stripes in a baby's room is a great way to have a little bit of fun without going overboard.

Classic furniture pieces add sophistication to a kid's room.

Mobile
furniture on
locking casters
maximize
bedroom
space.

BOY'S MASCULINE ROOM

I love kids' rooms that don't look too young but grow well with the child. Sally Wheat's son's room is masculine yet perfect for a young boy. Classic colors and textures work well here. Gray paint, stripes, dark brown leather, and a sophisticated sisal rug are truly timeless. And the rock 'n' roll artwork definitely ups the cool factor.

INGREDIENTS

Dark Gray Paint
Striped Paint Treatment
Sea Grass Carpet
Gray and White Rug
Metal Bunk Bed
Pillows
Desk
Reupholstered Chair
Rolling Nightstand
Lamp
Industrial Pendant
Framed Album Covers

RECIPE

STEP 1: Choose a cool dark gray for the walls to make a masculine statement fitting for a young man.

STEP 2: Adding a bold, striped metallic paint treatment on the ceiling gives instant visual interest. By selecting a sophisticated color scheme, you have a room that grows with the child.

STEP 3: Select a kid-friendly, durable material like sea grass for the floor. The natural material and color give warmth to the otherwise cool color palette. Layering a playful patterned rug gives a stripe of color.

STEP 4: A metal bunk bed provides another sleeping area for sleepovers while saving much-needed space. Stacked beds also add an element of fun. Boys will love to flip a coin over who gets to sleep on top.

STEP 5: Storage, storage, storage! One can never have too much! A rolling nightstand provides mobility and space to tuck things away. Pair it with a masculine glass lamp.

STEP 6: When selecting artwork, consider unconventional objects. Not all art has to be for a kid. If he loves The Beatles, create a collage of small posters or pages of lyrics. Framed album covers in this room give a nod to family favorite Prince.

continued

STEP 7: A growing child's room always needs an adequate work space. Instead of going with a conventional desk chair, choose vintage and reupholster with a stylish, durable fabric.

STEP 8: Add striped sheets to mimic the ceiling and a bright pop of color with yellow pillows on the bed. The yellow complements the neutral color scheme and keeps it from feeling too blue.

STEP 9: Install brown rattan shades to add another texture to the windows.

STEP 10: Finish with an industrial hanging pendant to add the wow factor.

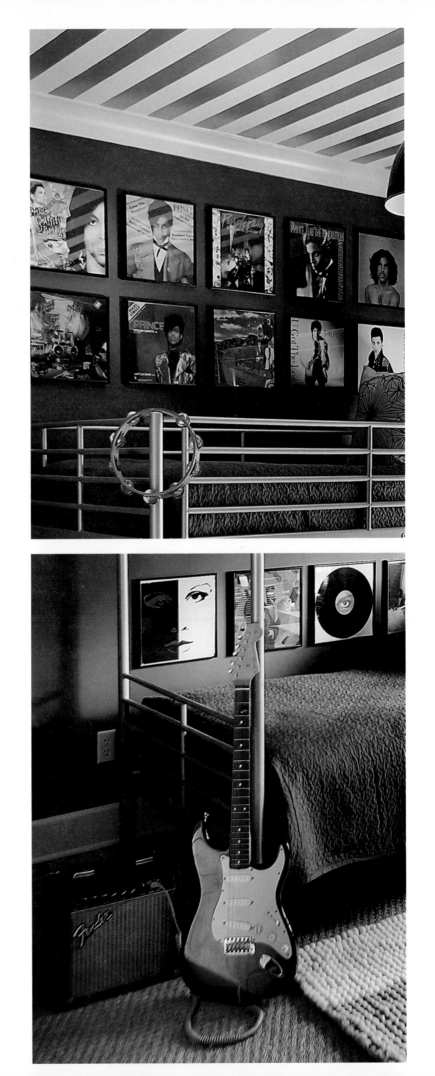

Have a little fun with storage in a kid's room. Lockers will hide all the toys and still look good when your child is in high school.

Make the nursery even lovelier by customizing window treatments. Dress up an inexpensive window panel with a band of another fabric on the bottom.

Old schoolhouse maps double as artwork.

Cool shapes in a kid's room make things more fun!

KRISTIN'S DIY CANOPY

For a little girl, there is nothing cooler than a canopy in her room. I remember I had one and would spend endless hours dancing to Madonna and Michael Jackson in it! So when I saw the one that Kristin Jackson made for her daughter, I thought, *I need to share this!* Now, much to my chagrin, I didn't have the gorgeous chandelier in my childhood room, but when and if I do have a little girl, this is going up!

INGREDIENTS

3 Colors of Fabric
Four-by-Eight Sheet of Plywood
Light Kit
Fabric Strips
Wood Screws
2 Two-by-Fours

TOOLS

Staple Gun and Staples
Table Saw or Skill Saw
Saw Horses
Chisel
Drill and Drill Bits
Painter's Tape
Stud Finder
Sewing Machine or Stitch and Witch
Fabric Panels*

*Fabric Panels (for use with a standard twin daybed and a standard crib bed skirt):

- Panel A: length from ceiling to floor with added hem allowance fifty-four inches wide.
- Panel B: length from ceiling to floor, including swag dimension, with added hem allowance fifty-four inches wide.
- Panel C: length from ceiling to floor, including swag dimension, with added hem allowance.
- Panel A and Panel B will all be the same orange fabric. Panel C will be your contrasting white fabric.

RECIPE

STEP 1: Precut your panels to the correct lengths, taking into account any fabric repeats and pattern matching. Once all the panels are cut, sew them all together using a standard stitch through your sewing machine. You will want the front of the fabric to always be facing the same direction, even with the white panels.

STEP 2: Cut your plywood to the interior dimension of your crib skirt. To add a chandelier to the interior of the canopy, add a small hole for the plug-in light kit. Use a skill saw and a chisel to notch out a place for the cord to lay once it is flush with the ceiling. This is completely optional.

continued

STEP 3: Attach your fabric. Attach an orange panel to your plywood panel using a staple gun, starting in the center and wrapping your way around. Your white panel will be hanging off the front for a minute. When you are stapling, gather little bunches together every few inches. This will allow for a full look once hung.

STEP 4: Next, take your white panel and wrap it back around what you have already stapled. This layer does not need to be gathered as much. Just make sure you leave yourself enough to wrap the back corner.

STEP 5: If you are using curtain panels that aren't long enough, make some fabric strips from some leftover fabric and use them as tabs. Staple them over the first orange fabric panel.

STEP 6: Once everything is stapled, trim up the tails and add the crib skirt. Cut off one of the long panels. (You don't need all that extra fabric hanging in the back.) Cut out the center lining, leaving the inside border to staple on.

STEP 7: Tape out the bed dimensions and then center the canopy dimensions on top of that. Determine where the rafters in the ceiling are. After marking those dimensions, make the pilot holes into the plywood. If your ceilings are eight feet tall, use two two-by-fours between the floor and the plywood to hold the canopy in place while you drill.

KID'S ROOM STARTERS AND SWEET TOUCHES

Kids' artwork doesn't have to look childish. Add a little rock 'n' roll. Frame albums as artwork in a bedroom.

Go with more of a sophisticated fabric. A futuristic geometric design is just more fun!

A gallery display of black-and-white family photos in matching frames keeps a kid's room from looking too cluttered.

TELEPHONE

VICKI'S DIY TELEPHONE BOOTH

How do you get your kids to put away their clothes? Tell them to put them in the telephone booth! I mean, really, isn't this the cutest thing you've ever seen? So easy to make, and all you need is some red paint and an eBay account! Vicki Eastland is a genius!

INGREDIENTS

Red Paint
Telephone Booth Sign

TOOLS

Paintbrush
Industrial-Strength Velcro
Pencil
Measuring Tape
Painter's Tape
Razor Blade
Glass Cleaner

RECIPE

STEP 1: Tape off the interior glass panels to avoid getting any paint on the glass.

STEP 2: Measure and mark the top of your telephone booth with a pencil.

STEP 3: Using the red paint, paint the door and the wall, forming a telephone booth.

STEP 4: Wait for paint to dry.

STEP 5: Scrape off any paint on the glass with a razor blade and some glass cleaner.

STEP 6: Attach the telephone booth sign with industrial-strength Velcro.

NOA'S DIY SPACE

Faith Blakeney believes that all kids should have a sacred space that's all theirs. A place that they can play in, read a book in, or relax in. So she took a small, unused space in her daughter's room and transformed it into her own little sanctuary. Here, she shares how you can create a space like this for your little one too.

INGREDIENTS

Soft, Non-Elastic Fabric
Upholstery Tacks

TOOLS

Hammer
Scissors
Pen
Pins

RECIPE

STEP 1: Measure each wall in your space. You will be cutting out one piece of fabric for each wall. Before you do this, add one inch around each side of the fabric (for a hem—no sewing involved).

STEP 2: Mark your fabric to delineate where you will be cutting it out. You may also want to mark your fabric (on the hem) to remind yourself which piece goes on which wall, if the walls are different dimensions.

STEP 3: Now cut out each piece. Fold the one-inch hem and pin it so it stays in place. Do this for each side of every piece of fabric. Once you are finished, take your first piece of fabric and place a tack into a top corner, half an inch from the top and side edges. Hammer the tack into the wall at the corner.

STEP 4: Take the opposite corner of the fabric and do the same, making sure that the fabric is as taut as possible. Repeat this with the other two corners. Now that your fabric is on the wall, attached by four tacks, measure the center of each piece of fabric, midway between the two tacks, and put a tack there, again as taut as possible. Repeat on all sides of fabric. You will want to repeat this step so that in the end you have tacks from eight to twelve inches apart around all edges of your fabric. Take out all pins. Repeat these steps for every piece of fabric, and you have an upholstered wall: a fundamental element for any sacred space!

living room

LIVING ROOM

When I was younger and visiting my grandparents, I noticed they covered their furniture in plastic. I remember thinking, *What's the point of having a couch you can't sit on?* Well, that's still how I feel. Why spend money on something if you can't enjoy it? Living rooms are meant to be lived in! Comfortable pieces should adorn the space, organization should be key, conversation pieces should be intermingled, and memories should be made. Period.

COMFORTABLE LIVING

- Find an inspiration piece. This could be a rug, artwork, or a sofa. Pull colors and textures from that piece to build your style. Always incorporate at least one or two neutrals to balance out the overall look of the space and tie in texture. Velvet, faux fur, silk, animal print, cotton, linen, and geometric prints are all great options for layering.

- When determining the look and style of your living room, try to avoid anything too trendy. Chances are it'll be out of style in a year or two, and then you'll have to go shopping again. Choose classic pieces that can be easily mixed and matched with other furniture pieces later on.

- Let the size of your space determine what furniture will work for you. Pieces that are too large can make the space feel cluttered and cramped. However, a few large pieces can lend balance and harmony to the room. Plants and bookcases are great choices for adding height, regardless of the room's size. My favorite piece for a living room is a chest of drawers, which offers storage and height at the same time.

- When choosing a sofa, always pick a classic neutral to build off of. Sofas don't have to cost a lot of money. You can dress them up with pillows for a high-end look. You should, however, buy one that will last for the next six to seven years. Do your research and find a sturdy one that fits within your budget. Depending on how big your family is, sectional sofas can be a great option that affords ample space. If you have kids and pets in the house, opt for hands-on fabrics and slipcovers that easily can be taken off and washed.

- Ground all your furniture pieces with a rug. This will create a zone that ties them together. This is also a great opportunity to incorporate patterns and color. For a polished look, the sofa and flanking chairs should always be either completely on or completely off the floor rug. The larger the rug in a small space, the bigger the room will look.

- Coffee tables come in every shape and size imaginable. Try to mix and match shapes in your living room for variety. A round glass table will not only make your space look and feel bigger, but it also contrasts powerfully with dark, boxy furniture. Wood coffee tables are a great idea if you're looking for something more substantial or if you need your coffee table to double as storage. If space is limited, go for several smaller tables or try ottomans that can be moved around the room.

- Combine old or heirloom pieces with modern pieces for an eclectic and cohesive feel. Explore thrift stores, flea markets, and estate sales for pieces that will add character to your living room. If you see a piece you like but can't stand the fabric or color, consider reupholstering or painting it.

- For years designers have been trying to find ways to conceal the television, but the days of the bulky TV are over. If you're going to keep the television in your primary living space, there are numerous ways to place it so it's not in your direct eye line. You can mount it on the wall and surround it with pieces of art so it blends in or paint the wall a darker color so it disappears. You can also conceal it behind doors or put it in the center of shelves so that it just fades away. In a smaller space, opt for a sleeker, low-slung television to keep everything streamlined. A console under the television works well to hide DVDs and remotes.

- Accent tables are great if you need extra surface space. The height should be the same as the arm of your sofa or chair and large enough to accommodate a lamp and a few glasses.

- To maximize the room's potential, lighting should be tailored to the space and a variety of lighting sources should be used. Conventional lighting, like recessed cans, work well for overhead task lighting while floor and table lamps can be placed around the room to create zones. Lastly, sconces work well flanking a fireplace or illuminating a bookcase. It's okay to have dark corners in a space, but use at least two light sources to give the room an inviting glow.

- Art is an important way to incorporate color or inject personality in a space. Get creative here. Blow up a photograph, paint an abstract piece of art, or frame images from your favorite book. Don't be afraid to play with scale. A large piece over a sofa can make a bold statement and tie all the colors of the room together.

- Strategically accessorize. If it looks like too much, it is too much. Your coffee table should look like a piece of art.

- Be sure to include one bold conversation piece. Let your room have a story to tell.

- Don't let everything sit against the wall. Allow a few of your furniture pieces to float.

- If you love to entertain, go for an indoor/outdoor flow.

- Fill in the empty spaces, but don't clutter them. If you have an empty corner, add a plant or a tall round table with books and flowers. You could also add another chair and reading lamp or a banquette for extra seating.

Go with paint palettes that inspire you, especially in your living room.

Dress up a lonely corner with a table and some branches. Now it becomes a functional space with some character.

If you could splurge on one piece in the living room, focus on the sofa. A great sofa is invaluable!

Fake architecture with lighting. An arched swing arm wall sconce is much better than overhead lighting for a living room, and it adds a bit of charm to the space.

Offset the television in a living room to conceal it.

For high style in your living room, go for unique pieces that mix cool materials like these amazing bamboo and Lucite chairs. Choose pieces that are on wheels for easier mobility.

KID-FRIENDLY

Beth Dotolo of Pulp Studios wanted to create a space that was welcoming to kids and pets but still had designer touches. The trick: incorporating high and low pieces. When designing for a family, you don't have to throw all your designer tricks away. You just have to know how and where to use them.

INGREDIENTS

Family-Friendly Sofa
Large Ottoman for a Coffee Table
Credenza for Television
Large Rug
Bright Wire Chair
Custom-Made Pillows

Velvet Commercial-Grade Pillows
Floor Lamp
Artwork
Coffee Table Tray
Conversation Piece

RECIPE

STEP 1: Start with what you have. Especially when working on a budget, assess your pieces and work around them first. The homeowners in this case already had a sofa, a loveseat, and an ottoman in good shape, so they worked around them. Soft, round edges are also a must when creating a family space. The softer the better.

STEP 2: Go with a rug that is bold but that works for the whole family. Pick something bright and fun but livable.

STEP 3: Give a plain sofa some life. Mix custom pillows with an inexpensive sofa to add luxury. Velvet always does the trick. You can always go with commercial grade. They look fragile, but they aren't.

STEP 4: This is a family space, so love the television. Anchor it by adding a beautiful credenza. After all, it's functional and this is a modern age.

STEP 5: Bring in bright, bold colors in the other seating elements. You can substitute ottomans for sitting chairs as well. They are easily movable and great for storage.

STEP 6: Use art that you have. If it means something to you and tells a story, why not use it?

STEP 7: Add functional accessories. A tray on the top of the ottoman gives the kids a place to play and do puzzles.

STEP 8: Always add one conversation piece. It doesn't have to be designed into the space. Things can be coordinated around it.

STEP 9: Remember this is a family space. Everything should tell a story of who you and your family are.

BETH'S DESIGNER TIP: If you're going to splurge, pick one great piece and make sure it's right for you. You can mix inexpensive pieces around it to make it look even more luxurious.

An abstract art piece can bring all the colors of the room together, while a leaning photo is a more casual approach to displaying artwork.

Benches are great extra seating. A vintage bench reupholstered in leather keeps the look modern and exciting.

In a large room, go for a rug that pulls the whole room together. As an added touch, paint the insets of the bookcases the same color to make the room look like it extends deeper than it already does.

In a studio with high ceilings, install a curtain rod. It's a soft and easy way to separate the spaces.

CONVERTIBLE STUDIO

Studio spaces are tough to contend with. You never have enough storage, and you always seem to be having a dinner party in what essentially is your bedroom. Brooklyn Home Company transformed an ordinary studio into a place where you could comfortably do all of that without having your guests sit on your bed. By using store-bought pieces and reclaimed materials from other jobs, they turned a studio into a budget-friendly, ready-made entertaining space.

INGREDIENTS

White Cotton Sofa
Blue Graphic Print Rug
Brushed-Nickel Coffee Table
White Console
White Lamps
Wood Beams
Bed Base with Built-in Storage
Paper Light Fixture
Lath Divider
Handmade Art
Wall Mirror

RECIPE

STEP 1: Buy double-duty furniture. A store-bought bed base with storage is crucial in a small space. With limited room to store things, this is a perfect place to start.

STEP 2: Create a division in the space. Here, a lath from old construction jobs was used as a divider. The wood warms up the space and provides privacy but eliminates the heavy divider feeling. To make your own wood lath divider, run a few pieces of lath vertically and nail the remaining pieces horizontally. Attach it to the bed surround for complete privacy. Experiment with the colors as well. A mixture of white paint and water gives these planks a whitewash finish to match the rest of the room.

STEP 3: Add texture and color with a floor rug in a graphic print. Here, the colors from the lath are extended with a light blue rug to ground the living space and tie the two spaces together.

STEP 4: Choose an inexpensive slipcovered sofa for the living area. It's easy to wash, budget-friendly, and gives you the option of changing the color later without sacrificing your wallet.

STEP 5: Opt for a leggy brushed-nickel coffee table instead of a heavy wood one. Light and airy, the table can be easily moved. The reflective metal finish is good for bouncing the light around the room and making it feel larger.

continued

STEP 6: Add a console to conceal the bedding area and to provide a surface space for additional lighting and storage. A small bowl on top is a great catchall for keys and sunglasses when you walk through the door.

STEP 7: Install a sculptural paper chandelier for additional overhead lighting and a mirror behind the sofa to dress up the space and reflect the light.

STEP 8: Treat the lath as an additional wall and personalize the space with artwork made locally. A piece by an artist who specializes in felt marker prints is a perfect choice for such a small space.

Go for a simple presentation on the fireplace to show off the beauty of your pieces.

Create
interesting
ceilings.
Consider them
your fifth wall.

NEUTRAL READING ROOM

In a wide-open reading room that also acts as your primary living room, you want to make sure you have lots of neutral comfortable fabrics, interesting pieces, and ample lighting. Erin Martin, an interior designer in St. Helena, California, designed an architectural marvel for two Francophiles. True to form, she outfitted it with interesting historical details, serene textures, plenty of reading lights, and two great sofas to curl up on.

INGREDIENTS

Gigantic Moroccan Rug
2 White Linen Sofas
European Chandelier
Marble Coffee Table
Brushed-Nickel Reading Lamps
Library Ladder
Mirror Made from an Old Building Remnant
Library Sconces
Custom-Built Cabinetry

RECIPE

STEP 1: Start by painting the walls a neutral color to unify the whole space. In a room this size, you want to make the room feel as if everything relates to each other. Keeping a consistent palette will make everything feel more organic.

STEP 2: The trick here is to not worry about hiding your television. If this is your living space, you should feel free to leave it out. If budget isn't a concern, have some custom bookcases made to house it. You won't even realize it's there.

STEP 3: Ground the entire space with a rug. To create a zone in a great room, make sure the rug is large enough to fit both sofas and the coffee table on. Choosing a neutral rug with a subtle pattern will soften the space but still give the floors some interest.

STEP 4: Incorporate two white linen sofas that will flank the fireplace. The color is soft and serene to keep the room light and more intimate, whereas a darker sofa would've made the room feel heavier.

STEP 5: Create a coffee table from interesting pieces. In this case, the coffee table is a Calcutta marble top resting on top of a 1950s base.

STEP 6: Here, an artist was hired to do subtle artwork. The fireplace façade has the first lines of the owners' favorite books stenciled on it. The subtle paint colors add interest without being distracting.

continued

STEP 7: Incorporate lighting. Lighting is imperative in a reading room. In an architectural space like this, make sure your lighting matches the overall aesthetic. Architecturally interesting reading lights sit on either side of the sofa, while library sconces placed about the bookcase highlight the area. For additional lighting, bring in a chandelier that is substantial enough for the size of the room but also brings in that rustic vibe.

STEP 8: Bring in vintage accessories with a story. A mirror made from remnants of an old building and an old library ladder are functional and decorative.

STEP 9: As a finishing touch, cover all the books in brown paper and handwrite the titles. The look is more artistic and lends itself to the neutral palette in the room.

Graphic print rugs are like floor art. Pair with a glass coffee table for a bigger impact and some texture in your space.

WEEKEND RETREATS

decor

Mix up the shapes and styles of your tables. A simple but stylish accent table works well in any room.

jurgen peters

mixed-media, ltd.
chicago

ECLECTIC AND COLORFUL

Bohemian and beautiful, this space Justina Blakeney created is eclectic and colorful. To be honest, I channel my inner wannabe hippie when I see this room, and I just want to play my Janis Joplin albums over and over again. I love the mix of textures and colors that work so well together. These bright, bold colors and patterns are pleasing and comfortable.

INGREDIENTS

L-shaped Sectional
Vintage Kilim Pillows
Ikat Pillows
Solid-Colored Throw Pillows
Vintage Graphic Rug
Sheepskin-Covered Stool

Rustic Wooden Coffee Table
Plants
Graphic Midcentury Artwork
Funky Chandelier
Mirrors
Metallic Animal Sculptures

RECIPE

STEP 1: Start with white walls to make room for other colors in the space. Put more focus on two or three colors, such as the pops of orange found throughout this room in the form of throw pillows and artwork. This helps create a visual coherence so that everything in the room, even items from very different periods in very different styles, all look great together.

STEP 2: Add a simple sectional and rustic coffee table plain enough to let the colorful graphic rug pop. Feel free to drape pretty textiles over your couch. Besides adding texture, it's an easy way to freshen up the look of a couch that you may be tired of.

STEP 3: Funky artwork and a hodgepodge of throw pillows bring in an eclectic mix of colors and styles. Always stick with a simple color palette of two or three colors with varying graphic prints for a cohesive look.

STEP 4: Incorporate interesting details, such as these gold ceramic elephants, the pompom chandelier, and the sheepskin-covered stool (an easy DIY), which add texture to the space.

STEP 5: Bring the outdoors in with plants, and add vintage mirrors to reflect light and make the space feel larger.

JUSTINA'S DESIGNER TIP: If you find a cute stool but don't like the upholstery, buy it! Use faux sheepskin to reupholster the little stool. This one is a great little piece that cost less than twenty dollars to put together.

Painting the walls and the molding the same color makes the room look bigger, especially when using a dark color. Skipping the white molding makes the room look as though it has no boundaries.

Liven up neutral tones in a living room with bright artwork and textiles in great shapes!

Nowhere in the entertaining handbook does it say your glassware has to be clear. These will ensure a colorful cocktail party!

CHIC BACHELOR

Nicole Cohen, blogger and artist, had a blank canvas to work with, and the bachelor living here let her do whatever she wanted. She was going for reflective, soft, hard, sculptural, uncluttered, and powerful and wanted each piece to hold its own. I'm assuming after the transformation, this bachelor is now a chick magnet!

INGREDIENTS

Emerald-Green Custom Sofa in Brushed Cotton
Black-and-White Rug
Polished Steel Coffee Table
Lucite and Rattan Chairs
Lucite Side Table
White Kitchen Table
Orange Chairs with Zebra-Print Upholstery
Sculptural Chandelier
White Entry Table
Faux Tom Dixon Lamp
Faux Fur Throw
Black-and-White Graphic Pillows
Black Blinds
Entryway Mirror
Letter Holder
Key Holder

RECIPE

STEP 1: Choose white for your walls for a clean palette in the living room. Because this is a bachelor pad, Nicole wanted to limit the color palette and stick to the main pieces. To make the entryway stand out, however, she went for a Kelly Wearstler–inspired look by freehand painting a black graphic on the wall. In the small space, it separates the entry from the living room but still ties both rooms together.

STEP 2: Create a sense of luxury. Use high and low materials to create a more expensive look. Start with your floor rug. A black-and-white shag rug brings in texture.

STEP 3: A custom-made brushed-cotton sofa gives the room the main jolt of color but doesn't overwhelm. Go with a jewel tone like emerald green, which is feminine, masculine, and seductive at the same time.

STEP 4: Go for extra seating with Lucite and rattan sitting chairs. Choose ones that are appropriate for the size of the space, fit comfortably, and are on wheels so your guests can move around.

continued

STEP 5: Rather than a glass table, which would get lost in the space, go for a polished steel coffee table that reflects the light and the pieces on it. It's a glamorous version of glass.

STEP 6: Black-and-white throw pillows and a faux fur blanket soften the space and increase the opulence factor.

STEP 7: Install a black sculptural chandelier to echo the graphic black-and-white wall. Keep it simple. You want something with shape, but you don't want it to look too busy.

STEP 8: Go for dining furniture with shape to complement the very sculptural chandelier. Orange, curved chairs with zebra-print upholstery connect to the dominant colors of the room while still bringing in an additional color.

STEP 9: Keep the window treatments masculine by installing simple black slat blinds.

STEP 10: Dress up the entryway with a small Parsons table, a faux designer lamp, and a few catchalls.

Stack a fireplace with unused books during the spring and summer months. To give it more of a rustic and uniform feel, face all the spines inward.

Put your sofa on wheels. Turn it toward the fireplace to entertain; turn it toward the television for movie night.

A knockoff designer lamp can look just as good as the original for a fraction of the cost. Now you can have more money to invest in the rest of the room.

SYMMETRICALLY BEAUTIFUL

Sally Wheat's living room looks like a Carrie Bradshaw gown: soft and impeccably decorated. It's perfectly balanced, layered, and accessorized. It maintains a formal aesthetic, yet because of the use of so many great textures it's not stuffy. What I especially love about this room is that by simply changing out one ticket item like the rug or the throw pillows, you can create a whole new classic and well-tailored look for little money.

INGREDIENTS

White Paint
Velvet Sofa
Suede Vintage Chairs
Mirrored Coffee Table
Sea Grass Rug
Cowhide Rug
Lamps
Lucite Side Table
Gold and Glass Vintage Wheat Side Table
Mongolian Fur Chrome Benches
Pair of Painted Side Tables
Antique Gilt Mirror
Pillows
Vintage and New Accessories
Sheer Linen Drapes
Large-Scale Modern Abstract Art

RECIPE

STEP 1: Color can be powerful in small doses. Start with a neutral white palette on the walls, and the colors with subdued tones will have an impact. Add a soft color, such as lilac, to a neutral scheme for a subtle burst of personality. This color will pop, especially when used against a good white wall.

STEP 2: Add a floor rug. A natural cowhide placed on top of a sea grass rug allows the eye to move around contrasting fibers and gives the floor layers.

STEP 3: Choose a mirrored coffee table or Lucite table to trick the eye. It's almost as if it's not there and adds just the right amount of glamour.

STEP 4: Add a darker sofa to give the room depth. Choose one in a luxurious velvet material. Velvet always makes things look and feel more expensive.

continued

STEP 5: Pairs of items have huge impact and create symmetry throughout the space. Two vintage club chairs or two modern stools are so much better than one and make the space interesting. Using more than one style of chair keeps the room from looking too repetitive.

STEP 6: In lieu of art, use mirrors. Mirrors make a room appear bigger, especially when placed at one end of the room, and can mimic the look of a window. Be conscious of where you place a mirror, though. Make sure that what it reflects is desirable.

STEP 7: Accessorize strategically to break up monotony. A symmetrical layout can be boring, but it doesn't have to be. By sprinkling vintage and new accessories throughout the space, you can create interest and make the eye dance around these special moments.

STEP 8: For a very subtle design palette, layer texture and pattern. Fur covering a chrome-legged stool adds tons of life. Likewise, a leopard pillow adds an interesting pattern to the sofa.

STEP 9: Don't be afraid to mix your metals! Gold and silver coexist beautifully. Use vintage when possible. One-of-a-kind furniture pieces and accessories make a space unique and memorable. Always try to mix vintage, antique, and new to create interest and make your rooms sing.

STEP 10: Incorporate large-scale art to add drama and tie the color scheme together. Art can be a great starting point for any room.

Instead of one art piece, play up the vertical space in the room with multiple small pieces using the same subject.

Theatre seats against a wall offer an unconventional seating option when friends come over.

Display family photos in a whole new way. Enlarge your favorite photo for a gigantic wall mural.

Give a classic style like this wingback chair a modern makeover. Reupholster it in fur fabric for a conversation piece.

AMBER'S DIY
SUZANI COFFEE TABLE

An upholstered ottoman has two uses: seating and surface space. Inject some personality into your space with a suzani and an old ottoman. Easy breezy as it gets!

INGREDIENTS

Suzani
Old Upholstered Ottoman
Upholstery Tacks

TOOLS

Scissors
Hammer

RECIPE

STEP 1: Measure the top and sides of your ottoman.

STEP 2: Cut the suzani to fit over the top and sides with three inches to spare on either side to be able to fold the fabric in on the edges about an inch.

STEP 3: Using the upholstery tacks, tuck the fabric underneath so you can't see the cut side, and tack the fabric into the bottom side of the ottoman.

STEP 4: Do all four sides first and do the corners last to ensure the proper fitting.

STEP 5: For the corners, fold over as if you are making a corner of a bed and tuck in.

Home & Garden

Dress up the insides of old cabinets with stencils to make them more interesting.

Tongue-and-groove paneling on the wall painted a deep green warms up the space. A perfect solution for incorporating color, texture, and style.

Embrace happy accidents. This thrifted planter now has a new life with a quick coat of spray paint!

KRISTIN'S DIY SKIRTED CONSOLE

Everyone at one time or another would love to hide all the television components and wires. Using a curtain panel and some grosgrain ribbon, you can create a console of your own.

INGREDIENTS

MDF Cut to Size of Desired Top
Paint for MDF
1 Curtain Panel, Fifty-Six Inches by Ninety-Eight Inches
Grosgrain Ribbon
Fabric Glue
Hem Tape

TOOLS

Staple Gun

RECIPE

STEP 1: Paint the tops and sides of your MDF panel and set aside to dry.

STEP 2: Measure out the length of each of your fabric panels, including allowance for hem.

STEP 3: Using the hem tape (or a sewing machine), create a clean hem around each separate panel.

STEP 4: Using the fabric glue, attach your grosgrain ribbon trim to each separate panel.

STEP 5: Measuring the distance to the floor, use a staple gun to attach each panel to the underside of the MDF panel, attempting to get as close to the edge as possible.

STEP 6: Allow for a few extra strips of fabric, roughly eight inches wide, to be attached on top of the fabric panels. These will act as the fabric tongues between the slits or pleats.

STEP 7: Flip your piece right-side-up and place on your existing shelf or console unit.

A well-styled rustic table creates an instant well-dressed bar in a living room.

Add interesting accessories. Bookends bring some shelf appeal and turn literature into small collections.

To make a statement in a living room, paint one piece a bold color.

Hanging artwork on either side of the television makes the television appear to be part of the art installation.

LEAH'S DIY STAMPED RUG

Everybody has stenciled, but has everybody stenciled with a doormat? This is a great way to customize a rug for your living room and incorporate extra color. A little bit of paint and a rubber mat can add a graphic print to an inexpensive rug.

INGREDIENTS

Large-Scale Floor Rug
Rubber Doormat
Latex Wall Paint
Water

TOOLS

Paint Roller and Paint Tray
Large Drop Cloth
Paintbrush

RECIPE

STEP 1: Place your large-scale rug on the drop cloth.

STEP 2: In a large paint tray, mix latex paint and water until you get a desired consistency and color. You can play with the variations here, depending on how dark you want your stencil to be.

STEP 3: Using the paint roller, roll the paint over the rubber doormat.

STEP 4: Using the doormat as a stencil, press the doormat paint-side-down onto the rug.

STEP 5: Continue until you have covered the entire rug. Try not to overlap your pattern.

LORI'S DIY EYELASH ART PIECE

I love interesting art, and I think this piece Lori purchased is ingenious! Art made from false eyelashes! The cool part is that it brought texture to the walls where there wasn't any. Conceptually imaginative, this is definitely a conversation piece.

INGREDIENTS

Shadow Box
Heavy Stock Craft Paper or Poster Board
Double Stick Tape
False Eyelashes
Glue

TOOLS

Scissors

RECIPE

STEP 1: Cut poster board to the size of the shadow box.

STEP 2: Super glue false eyelashes randomly onto the paper until you have the desired look.

STEP 3: Use double stick tape to attach the art piece to the shadow box.

STEP 4: Put on the top of the shadow box and hang.

bathroom

BATHROOM

Practical, functional, and durable: all terms I think of when designing a bathroom. The great news is that because of its smaller size, you can experiment a bit. The staples of the bathroom never change, but the design scheme can be a bit more fun to tackle. Brilliant whites, alluring textiles, wall-to-wall tiles, decorative mirrors, and unique fixtures are just a few options for your oasis. This is a good place to splurge on the staples and indulge in the inexpensive luxuries.

RECIPE FOR A BATHROOM

- Before you start your bathroom renovation, set your budget and do your research. You can do a makeover on a small budget, but once you start getting into a demolition, things add up and you spend more than you anticipated. Look through magazines and books for inspiration and things that fit within your parameters.

- Begin with your walls. As far as color goes, lighting is key. If you choose a dark color, make sure you have ample lighting so it doesn't feel cave-like. Of course, you can never go wrong with neutrals. They never go out of style and you can always bring in color with your towels, a shower curtain, and accessories. When painting, remember to always use semigloss paint in the bathroom. It's resistant to moisture and easier to clean.

- If you have a powder room and want to use wallpaper, go for it. However, if this is your primary bathroom with a shower and bathtub, it's smarter to avoid wallpaper and stick with paint to avoid ruining the walls with moisture.

- Bead board or tile in a bathroom can bring in texture and color and can be a great alternative to paint. A full wall of bead board gives a traditional look. In a smaller bathroom, penny tiles can make the room look bigger, whereas marble and subway tiles are always classic choices and will look good for the next ten years. How much tile you use will depend on your budget. Doing a full wall of tile can be very dramatic and look amazing if done right.

- When choosing fixtures, make sure you truly try it in the store before you buy it. See how it feels. For the shower or bathtub, it's always nice to have a handheld showerhead for easier cleaning. It also becomes really convenient when bathing children or pets. Depending on the other fixtures in the space, a consistent finish gives a cleaner look to the bathroom. Try to keep everything relatively the same.

- As far as your permanent fixtures go, white is the most practical color for sinks, bathtubs, and toilets. There are alternatives, but white will look good ten years from now.

- When choosing a sink, think of the layout of the space and your needs. If the room is small, go for a washstand or a pedestal sink to save precious floor space. If you are looking for more storage, a full vanity is the way to go. You can have open shelving on the bottom and add baskets and towels, or you can choose a vanity with doors to conceal all your personal items.

- Carefully choose countertops for your vanity and other surfaces. Bring home a sample and test how it works in the space. Go with a material that fits your lifestyle and budget. Again, think long-term here. You can't go wrong with the classic Silestone, honed granite (matte), or marble.

- Toilets are available in all kinds of shapes and sizes. Some are energy efficient and conserve water. If you are dealing with a tight space, stick with a smaller design style.

- If you're in the market for a new bathtub, this again is something you should try in the store before you buy. Every tub is different. Some are deeper and wider than others, which will cause you to use a lot more water. Be conscious of how much water it will take to fill the tub so you won't see your water bill spike after you buy it. A claw-foot tub is a perfect suggestion for someone who wants to add a bit of character and charm. One with jets is perfect for a spa-like bathroom.

- A new shower stall can do wonders for a bathroom! It's such a big transformation. There are a few routes you can go. You can buy a prefab shower unit or a tiled unit. This will require either an experienced DIYer or your handy tile guy. As far as doors go, my favorites are the frameless shower doors. They have a cleaner finish and look almost invisible. If you have the space, consider separating the shower from the bathtub. Your bathroom will have a much more modern look. Of course, on a budget, you can always go with a shower curtain that will soften up the space and look just as fantastic.

- Flooring is another important component in a bathroom. This is certainly a place where things can get slippery when wet, so it's smart to avoid any polished surfaces, such as ceramic or porcelain. Mosaic tiles are a better choice because they are water resistant and the tiny grout lines offer some traction. Wood flooring typically isn't recommended because the water can get into the cracks and could eventually become moldy. Another alternative is vinyl. There are some great vinyl pieces out there that look like wood but are water resistant. If you do choose to use wood, teak and bamboo are great options. Lastly, cork tile is mildew resistant and soft on your feet.

- Correct lighting is imperative in a bathroom because it is such a small space. You want to make sure the lighting is both functional and appealing. Installing wall sconces on either side of the mirror or above is great for task lighting. I'm not a big fan of overheads, but if you are in the market for one, go for something interesting like a lantern or chandelier. Installing dimmers is a great way to turn your bathroom into a spa.

- Mirrors in a bathroom do double duty. They not only give you a place to do your hair but also make the room look bigger, which is important in such a small space. Frameless bathroom mirrors can look boring, so go for one that has a beveled edge or a frame. Find a frame you like at a thrift store or frame shop and have a piece of glass put into it. Generally, if you want more of the traditional look, go for something oval.

For a modern look, you can choose round or square. For storage, select a medicine chest and, if possible, see if it can be recessed into the wall so it doesn't look so bulky in the room.

- Storage is a must in a bathroom. Utilize every space you can. If possible, create niches between studs and add shelving. This is an underutilized space that can give you extra storage that you didn't even know was there.

- Last but not least, if you are in need of a small makeover on a limited budget, a fresh new set of towels, some new knobs, a rug, shower curtain, and accessories will typically do the trick. For more of a spa-like experience, simply change out the showerhead. Truly, it's the little things that count!

In a bathroom for more than one person, add a bit of farm character by using a trough sink. Perfect for kids, this throwback gives everyone a space to get cleaned up and leaves room for storage below.

Moorish blue tile work elegantly patterned in a small bathroom can turn the small space into an exotic retreat.

Play up the nautical theme in the bathroom by throwing in a blue and white shower curtain.

Large-print black-and-white wallpaper in a bathroom is graphic and gorgeous!

BARCELONA BATH

There is something about black-and-white bathrooms that I love, and you've probably gathered that if you've been flipping through this chapter. Now typically I prefer white grout, because it feels cleaner to me, but this bathroom is different. It has an edginess that only black grout can bring. I love the contrast in the space and, of course, the beautiful Kate Moss isn't too shabby to look at either.

INGREDIENTS

White Tile
Black Grout
Hexagon Mosaic Tiles in a Flower Pattern
Small Square Ceramic Tiles
Marble Console with Under-Mount White Sink
Brushed-Nickel Wall-Mounted Faucet
Wall Mirror
Art Deco Sconces
Large Black-and-White Kate Moss Print

RECIPE

STEP 1: Install the marble countertop first. Use one that has a pretty big reveal at the front to avoid being able to see the under-mounted sink. Not to mention, the thicker the slab, the more expensive the piece will look. Install a wall faucet when you are dealing with minimal space between the back edge and the wall. In my opinion, it just looks cooler!

STEP 2: Go for subway tile on the walls from floor to ceiling for the biggest impact. For the baseboards, use tile instead of wood to keep the tile theme. Go with little one-by-one white ceramic. In a room with a lot of foot traffic, it's always smarter to go with black grout to avoid being able to see the discoloration of the white grout over time.

STEP 3: Complete your tiling by using black-and-white hexagon tiles in a flower pattern on the floor. Going with black instead of white gives a nice contrast to the walls and grounds the room.

STEP 4: Accessorize. Add a wall mirror. Bring in art deco lights, which give the room a more modern feel. A large black-and-white print in a black frame pops off the white subway tile wall.

For extra storage, use the space above the toilet. Paint the back a darker color to give the shelves the illusion of more depth.

Hang a mirror with rope from the ceiling when wall space is minimal.

Use a full-wall mirror to make a small bathroom look twice its size.

OLD WORLD

I love the Old World feeling of this bathroom. The classic black-and-white theme with gold accents is oh, so charming. Above all else, it was the little details I noticed the first time I saw this room. The light fixture, the chair, the gold cart: these are all enduring ingredients that make this room.

INGREDIENTS

Black-and-White Hexagon Tile
Pedestal Sink
Gold Fixtures
Gold Shower Curtain Rod
Black-and-White Shower Curtain
Ornate Black Mirror
Black Claw-Foot Bathtub
Embossed Paintable Wallpaper
Chair Rail

Floor Molding
Marble Shelf with Black Brackets
Gold Cart
Old World Light
Black Chair
Gold Wall Extension Mirror
Black Stool
White Paint

RECIPE

STEP 1: Start by painting the walls a crisp white.

STEP 2: Wallpaper the lower half of the wall with an embossed paintable paper to add an extra texture to the space. Adhere it with wallpaper paste about three-quarters of the way up the wall. To finish the look, nail a small piece of molding to the top edge to create a chair rail.

STEP 3: Any Old World bath needs an old floor pattern to drive home the aesthetic. Install black-and-white hexagon tiles on the floor to bring in the black-and-white motif.

STEP 4: A gold circular ceiling-mounted curtain rod is great for encasing the tub, while a black-and-white shower curtain keeps the classic theme going.

STEP 5: Hang a shelf to set your incidentals on when you need them. A piece of marble can make a great shelf when hung with two inexpensive black brackets.

STEP 6: Add your accessories, such as a gold towel bar, extension mirror, stool, and chair. Stick with gold and black to keep the look consistent.

STEP 7: Bring in a gold cart for extra storage. This is helpful for storing extra towels and a few candles to allow the room to glow.

Instead of a typical bathroom door, make one using an old salvaged door, a track, and a few extra pieces of wood.

An ornate gold mirror, vintage wallpaper, and a chandelier with a cord cozy add charm in this petite interior.

GRAY AND WHITE CLASSIC

Jason Urratia's style is classic. He believes you should look at a room and love it every time. Case in point, this bathroom. While the style itself is timeless, he went for details that matter. The tile is extraordinary, the effect is brilliant, and the room is, well, amazingly classic.

INGREDIENTS

White Paint
White Vanity
Chrome Knobs and Pulls
Honed White Carrara Marble Countertop
Silver Vanity Mirror
Chrome Sconces
Handcrafted Gray Tile
White Subway Ceramic Tile
Black Tile
White Carrara Marble Floor Mosaic
Frameless Shower
Bathtub

RECIPE

STEP 1: To keep the room classic, start with white paint for the walls as your base.

STEP 2: Install your primary fixtures: your vanity, bathtub, and the half wall in the shower. For the vanity and shower divide, top it off with a white honed Carrara marble. Honed gives it more of a modern feel than glossy would.

STEP 3: Use white ceramic subway tile on both opposing walls. To give the room more dimension and keep it interesting, opt for a handcrafted gray tile on the back. It creates the illusion of depth and gives the appearance of an exterior wall. As a detailed touch, incorporate a small black tile.

STEP 4: Make the floors just as interesting. Honey-white Carrara mosaic lines the floors, while a Carrara border finishes the look.

STEP 5: A frameless glass shower keeps the room feeling open and airy and allows you to see the whole room even from the door.

STEP 6: Add simple lighting and accessories in chrome to reflect the light from the window and create a classic, gorgeous space.

The epitome of industrial modern, this vanity is mesmerizing to look at.

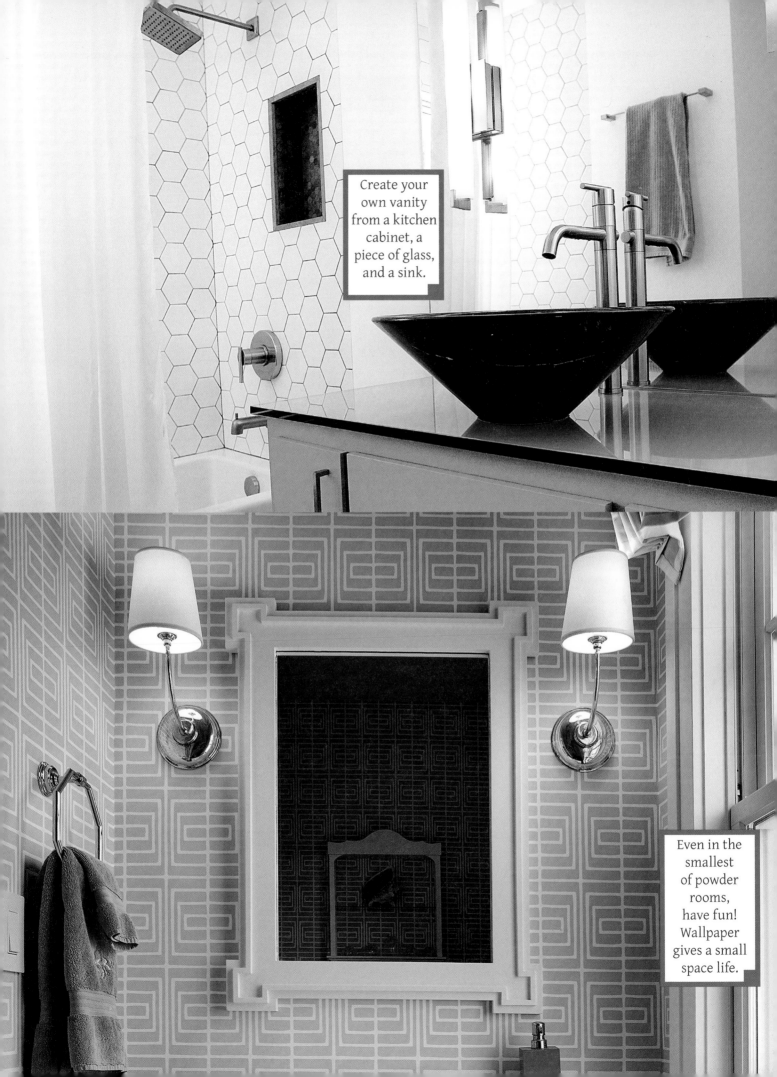

Create your own vanity from a kitchen cabinet, a piece of glass, and a sink.

Even in the smallest of powder rooms, have fun! Wallpaper gives a small space life.

HIS AND HERS

Lulu Powers knows how to cook, entertain, and decorate, and it's very evident when I look at her bathroom design. There are so many little details here. The room's feminine and masculine natures come out in the marble, wood, tile, and art. I love the way she used these materials to blend a his and hers bathroom so effortlessly.

INGREDIENTS

Light Blue Wall Paint
Subway Tile
Carrara Marble Top
Wood Bathtub Surround
Chrome Tub Faucet
Collected Art

RECIPE

STEP 1: Install bathtub and shower. Obviously these are the most important elements of the space. If you prefer more of a soaking tub, then go with something a bit bigger. An old-fashioned faucet gives the bathroom a vintage feel.

STEP 2: Go for crisp and clean subway tile. The classic nature makes it great for bathrooms because it will always look great. Only go halfway up the wall to create a backsplash for the bathtub.

STEP 3: Add a wood surround to the tub. For an aged look, consider staining it and wiping the stain off in places. It will give it a time-worn feel and make it look a bit more relaxed.

STEP 4: Start by painting the walls blue to mimic the look of water. If you have curved ceilings like the ones here, you can always go all the way up to the ceiling and around. Or you can stop at the break, as shown. Add a strip of molding at the paint break to define the ceiling and the wall. This is great to do when you have curved ceilings. Stain the piece of molding the same color as the bathtub surround to bring the color up to the wall as well.

STEP 5: Incorporate eclectic art. Here, Lulu stayed in the theme (water) but mixed up the subjects.

A great way to get a new countertop for half the price is to use a remnant instead of a full slab. Call around for remnants and have them cut for you.

An inexpensive piece of decorative paper attached with adhesive strips can easily dress up the inside of the medicine cabinet.

Your personal items look much more chic when placed on a silver vanity tray. Keep your collection limited to glass and silver for a stunning look.

WHIMSICAL BATH

Percy and Tara's bathroom is a charming and whimsical way to design. After all, who would've thought chalkboard paint would actually work in a bathroom? Its delicate and unconventional design is what makes this bathroom so wonderful. The best part? Every day you can draw yourself new wallpaper if you choose to!

INGREDIENTS

Chalkboard Paint for the Walls
Washstand
Hexagon Tiles for the Floor
Blue Paint for the Ceiling
White Paint for the Walls
Set of Wall Sconces
Wicker Wastebasket
Hand Towel
Chalk

RECIPE

STEP 1: Always start by painting the ceiling. That way any imperfections can be covered by your wall paint. Going with a blue ceiling color is a great alternative to harsh white and makes you feel like you could be outside.

STEP 2: Paint your side walls white. Paint your main focal wall with chalkboard paint. This is something you can buy at your local hardware store. If black isn't your color, however, you can make your own by mixing one-half cup of latex paint with one tablespoon of unsanded tile grout. You will have to adjust your paint-to-grout ratio depending on the size of your wall.

STEP 3: Using a period-specific tile on the floors brings even more whimsy. A 1920s hexagon shape with white grout is a perfect touch.

STEP 4: Introduce a little light into the space with wall sconces on either side of the sink.

STEP 5: Add minimal accessories, and draw away!

BATHROOM STARTERS AND SWEET TOUCHES

To give your bathtub an expensive makeover, splurge on the faucet and the surround. The higher the backsplash, the more expensive the tub will look.

Hide exposed pipes with a sink skirt. Do as my girlfriend Erica Islas suggests and use outdoor fabric. It's waterproof and mold resistant.

Keep everything looking effortless and monochromatic by hanging window treatments the same color as the wall.

Run dainty shelving along the wall to display candles and personal collections.

Accessorize the top of the toilet with a few small trinkets. A candle and small catchall keep even the obvious pieces decorated.

Industrial light fixtures, ornate mirrors, and vintage stools bring ample charm to a small bathroom.

For an open and airy feeling, go for a vanity with extra storage below and a built-in towel rack.

PRIVET
HOUSE
WARREN ORCHARD
with BLACK FIG
& HONEY

BEST IN TILE

Shapes and sizes can play a big role in your bathroom fixtures and materials. Depending on the size of your bathroom, you can get a pretty big bang for your buck. One of my favorite bathroom elements is tile. I just can't get enough of it. I've always insisted on using the smallest tile in small bathrooms because I do believe it gives the illusion of more surface space. Case in point, Bonnee Sharp created this bathroom using white penny tiles and gray wall tiles. I also love her use of the old and new by incorporating classic tile with a modern color and shape.

INGREDIENTS

Pair of Sconces
Overhead Light
Two-Piece Straight-Lined Pedestal Sink with Attached Towel Bar
Beveled Oval Vintage-Style Mirror
Widespread Faucet Set
Wall-Mount Soap Dispenser
Wall-Mount Cup Holder
Savoy Penny Rounds in Paperwhite
Gray Wall Tiles
Grout Mixed to Match Tiles on Floors and Walls

RECIPE

STEP 1: Start by creating a budget for your powder room. Kitchens and bathrooms can end up costing you a lot more money than you anticipated. Assess your walls and floor, vanity, lighting, and accessories. In a bathroom that is very tile heavy, your largest expense may come up there.

STEP 2: Install the white penny round tiles on the wall, continuing on to the floor.

STEP 3: When selecting a grout color, choose a dark one that matches your wall tile. The contrasting color makes the subway tiles on the floor pop and will eliminate dirty grout lines. It also gives the walls a smooth, seamless, modern look.

STEP 4: Choose a pedestal sink in a bright white with a contemporary no-frill contour. The chrome finish of the lav set should match any other metals used throughout the room. Alternatively, nickel finishes can be used if a warmer silver tone is desired.

STEP 5: Lighting should be similar in shape and simplicity to other elements in the room in order to complement the contemporary sink. Wall sconces should be hung evenly on either side of the mirror and just above average eye level. Choose sconces with enough power to provide sufficient light for makeup

continued

touch-ups, making sure the bulb is diffused or covered from line of sight. Frosted glass or a shielded bulb should always be used to avoid harsh lighting.

STEP 6: It's important that your accessories complement the metals, colors, and shapes used throughout the bathroom. Consider how the space will be used and who will most frequently inhabit it. Place sleek clean-lined wall-mount accessories a few inches higher than sink level to keep the items dry and within easy reach.

BONNEE'S DESIGNER TIP: Penny rounds not only evoke a bygone era but provide a safer nonslip surface when floors are wet. Using straight-lined subway tiles next to the retro penny rounds gives a nice contrast of eras, colors, and shapes. If long, narrow tile cannot be obtained, substitute subway rectangular-shaped tiles and lay them in a similar stacked pattern. White can be used for walls with a white grout for a brighter, lighter look in a room lacking windows.

For a cleaner look, use a track on your ceiling to hang your shower curtain.

A ladder leaning against the wall is a perfect towel rack.

Monogrammed Turkish towels give a personalized touch to any bathroom.

A cart used for a vanity offers storage and a built-in towel bar.

AGNES'S DIY BATHROOM MIRROR AND FRAME

Strolling through Bucktown in Chicago, I stopped at Buzz Coffee when I saw this mirror in the bathroom. It was a DIY bathroom project that the owner, Agnes, had made using raw lumber. What I love about this project is that everything except the mirror can be purchased inexpensively at any hardware store, it's easy to make, and you can even customize it by putting in a place to hold your towels if you wish!

INGREDIENTS

Mirror to Size Less Six Inches Horizontally from Total Size of Mirror Frame
6 Pieces of One-by-Four-Inch Lumber to the Overall Width of Mirror Frame
2 Pieces of One-by-Four-Inch Lumber to the Overall Height of Mirror Frame
1 Piece of One-by-Four-Inch Lumber for the Shelf, Four Feet Long
20 Three-Eighth-by-Two-Inch Bolts with Washers
1 Tube of Liquid Nails
7 Four-Inch Wood Screws

TOOLS

Stud Finder
Tape Measure
Marker
Drill
Saw
Wood Planer
Level
Three-Eighth-Inch
    Socket Wrench
Caulking Gun

RECIPE

STEP 1: Locate studs to establish the location for the mirror. (Studs are easily found at corners of walls.)

STEP 2: Plan for the left and right perimeters of the mirror to coincide with studs. Holes in the lumber must be drilled into the studs to support the frame and mirror.

STEP 3: Measure the distance between studs to establish the length of the boards side to side. The width of the glass should be six inches less than the length of the boards side to side. The height of the glass should be one inch more than will be visible.

STEP 4: Cut six boards to the desired overall length of the mirror.

STEP 5: Leave twenty-four inches of total space top to bottom for the panels in addition to the height of the glass section of the mirror.

STEP 6: Measure and mark the projected bottom height for the glass section of the mirror.

STEP 7: Measure eleven and a half inches below the projected bottom height of the glass section of the mirror, which will be the line for the bottom of the first board.

continued

STEP 8: Measure and mark one inch from the edges of both sides of the board and two inches from the bottom of both sides. Drill holes for three eight-inch bolts.

STEP 9: Hold the board in place and drill through the hole in the board into the stud.

STEP 10: Screw the bolt with the washer into the board and stud.

STEP 11: Level the board and repeat drilling and bolting on the other side.

STEP 12: Install the next board on top of the first the same way.

STEP 13: Plane the wall-facing edge of one side of the top board to create a one-fourth-inch by one-eighth-inch groove for the mirror along one edge.

STEP 14: Install the third board as you did the first two, with the groove facing up and toward the wall.

STEP 15: Liberally apply Liquid Nails to the back of the mirror and lift it into place with the bottom edge in the groove in the board and leaving three inches of clearance on each side of the mirror.

STEP 16: Plane the wall-facing edge of one side of the top board to create a one-fourth-inch by one-eighth-inch groove for the mirror on the top board.

STEP 17: Install the top board, as you did the others, with the groove over the mirror and facing the wall.

STEP 18: Plane one edge so it slips over the mirror.

STEP 19: Mount the verticals as you did the other boards.

STEP 20: For the shelf, cut two pieces at twelve inches each for the front pieces and four or five inches for the sides. Predrill holes and connect with washers, bolts, and Liquid Nails.

STEP 21: Measure and cut verticals to the distance between the top of the board below the mirror and the bottom of the board above the mirror.

STEP 22: Using any leftover lumber, screw a cleat to your existing wood frame and Liquid Nails and screw the box to the cleat to support it.

Incorporate two small shelves. It's a great place to store some of your personal items while accessorizing at the same time.

Decorate your bathroom as you would any other room. Use your favorite wallpaper and artwork. It could become your favorite room in the house!

In an awkward space, use a room divider instead of a shower door.

LEANNE'S DIY RUFFLED SHOWER CURTAIN

If you love to sew, then this DIY project from Leanne Barlow is for you. Granted, it can be a bit challenging, but these shower curtains can run you hundreds of dollars in the store. Taking the time to create one yourself can save you money and allow you to customize a shower curtain specifically for your bathroom!

INGREDIENTS

Shower Curtain or Three Yards of Sixty-Inch Cotton Fabric
10 Four-Yard Rows of Ruffles
Thread to Match Each Color
One-Fourth Yard of Lightweight Interfacing
Ruffle Foot

TOOLS

Sewing Machine
Scissors
Measuring Tape
Iron
Seam Ripper
Tailor's Chalk
Sewing Pins

RECIPE

STEP 1: Prewash all fabric before cutting and sewing. This way you can throw it in the wash when it gets dirty and not have to worry about it shrinking.

STEP 2: Cut your large piece of fabric to measure seventy and a half inches long by seventy-two and a half inches wide. (You might need to piece your fabric together to get these measurements.)

STEP 3: Cut a strip of fabric for the top of your shower curtain (where the shower curtain rings will go) that measures seventy-two and a half inches long by four and a half inches wide.

STEP 4: You will need ten ruffles total. Nine rows need to measure nine and a half inches long by one hundred forty-four inches wide. (This is double the width of the shower curtain to give you a nice full ruffle). The top row of ruffles needs to measure seven and a half inches long by one hundred forty-four inches wide. In order to get your strips that wide, stitch multiple strips together. The seams are barely visible once everything is ruffled. Note: You can group your ruffle colors any way you like. You can space them evenly and have two ruffles of each color. A nice effect is achieved when the colors aren't evenly spaced. Note that this shower curtain has two white ruffles, one cream, one light yellow, two medium yellow, three dark yellow, and one mustard. Tip: It helps to label each ruffle strip once everything is cut. Just pin a sticky note to each layer, numbering them from one to ten so that they get attached to the curtain correctly.

STEP 5: Surge/zigzag stitch around every edge of every piece of fabric: the main curtain, each ruffle, everything. You can take or leave this step, and it is super tedious, but you won't have to worry about your

continued

fabric ever fraying. Plus it will look professional. After putting so much work into a project, you want to make sure it will last you a long time.

STEP 6: Fold down and press the edges of your ruffles and sides of your main shower curtain body one-fourth inch. (Don't worry about the top thin piece to the main body.) Sew one-fourth inch away from the edge. Note: You don't have to fold under and sew the top of any of your ruffles. These won't be seen. Just the sides and the bottom will be.

STEP 7: Create the ruffle for the top strip of fabric. You can use your ruffle foot or stitch a long basting stitch and pull the end thread to create your ruffle manually. Sew it to the very top of your large main shower curtain body. (Make sure it is the seven-inch-long strip and not the nine-inch-long one.) Ensure it is the same width as your main curtain (seventy-two inches). This is easier said than done, but by the end of your sixth ruffle, you will be a master at manhandling one hundred forty-four inches of fabric.

STEP 8: Mark with tailor's chalk or a highlighter where each row of ruffles will be placed. Your main curtain length is seventy inches, and you have ten ruffles, so you will want seven inches of each ruffle showing. The top two inches of each ruffle (except for the very top row) will be hidden by the row of ruffles above it. Having the first row of ruffles helps give you an idea of where to start. Mark where your second row of ruffles will be sewn seven inches underneath your first row (remembering that the top two inches will be hidden). Then measure seven inches down from that mark for the third row, seven inches more for the fourth row, etc.

STEP 9: Ruffle the remaining nine strips of fabric. Make sure each row is seventy-two inches wide after being ruffled. Keep each row of ruffles labeled so you know in what order to place them.

STEP 10: Pin your ruffles to your main curtain along the lines that you have previously marked, and sew in place. Start by pinning about two rows at a time, sew them, then pin on two more rows. The more pins you use, the less chance your ruffles will shift as you are moving your fabric around. Note: The more ruffles that are attached, the heavier the fabric gets and the harder it is to control. So go slowly. Be constantly checking and double-checking that you don't have extra fabric bunched up under your needle as you sew.

STEP 11: Cut a strip of interfacing two inches wide by seventy-two inches long. (These can be pieced together if you don't have one solid strip long enough.)

STEP 12: Iron the top piece of your shower curtain in half width-wise, open it up, and place the interfacing in the middle. There should be about one-fourth inch of fabric that is not covered by the interfacing. Fold back in half and press long enough to make the interfacing bind to the fabric. Note: The interfacing will make the fabric more stable since buttonholes will be sewn along the top for your shower curtain rings.

STEP 13: Finish off the edges of the top of your shower curtain by folding in half wrong sides together, stitching one-fourth inch away from the edge, flipping right-side-out, and pressing.

STEP 14: Pin the top section of your shower curtain to the main body of the curtain, right sides together, with the bottom/raw edges pointing up. Stitch in place one-fourth inch away from the edge.

STEP 15: Fold the top of the shower curtain with the right side facing you, and press (make sure the edges in the back point down).

STEP 16: Sew buttonholes along the top strip of your curtain that you stabilized with the interfacing. Make sure your buttonhole is large enough to fit your curtain rings through. Tip: Try practicing on some scraps before you start so that you know exactly where to mark your fabric.

STEP 17: You will sew twelve buttonholes total. The two outside holes should be two inches away from each end; the rest of the buttonholes should all be six inches apart. Cut open each buttonhole with your seam ripper.

LEAH'S DIY ROPE MIRROR

Leah Moss is a DIY guru. She has so many great projects under her belt. I especially liked this one because it is easy and affordable. Hang this above a dresser or on a wall in a bathroom. It'll look fantastic wherever you place it.

INGREDIENTS

Stainless Steel Framed Mirror
Rope
Large Eye Hooks
Doorknob
Glue
3 Half-Inch Nails
Picture-Hanging Wire
Picture-Hanging Hook
Wax Cord

TOOLS

Drill
Hammer
Screwdriver

RECIPE

STEP 1: Attach heavy-duty picture wire to the back of the mirror, and secure a heavy-duty picture hook to the wall.

STEP 2: Hang the mirror, and measure half an inch on either side where you want each eye hook to go.

STEP 3: Measure one foot directly above the center of the mirror and mark the spot where you want the top of the rope to hit.

STEP 4: Take the mirror off the wall, predrill the holes, and then screw the eye hooks into the mirror.

STEP 5: Screw a regular screw into the wall at the place you marked for the top of the rope to hit.

STEP 6: Fill the cavity of an antique doorknob with glue and place it over the screw in the wall. (Purely decorative, the doorknob doesn't actually hold any weight, just masks the screw like a cover.)

STEP 7: Tie the rope to one eye hook, drape the middle section of the rope over the doorknob, gently pull the rope taut, then tie the other end of the rope to the remaining eye hook.

STEP 8: To ensure that it doesn't unravel, wrap black wax cord around the end of each knot.

STEP 9: Hang the mirror on the picture hook.

DeFOREST'S DIY GALVANIZED SHOWER SURROUND

Talk about designing for your surroundings! Inspired by industrial materials common on neighboring Iowa farms, DeForest Architects made this shower surround out of stock galvanized exterior siding. This is a great example of the urbanization of a rural surrounding. Leave it up to great architects to turn galvanized siding into a modern masterpiece!

INGREDIENTS

Galvanized Exterior Siding
Pole Barn Screws
Aluminum Flashing
Silicone Caulk
Liquid Nails
Sheet Metal (One-by-Three and a Light, Thin Piece)
Metal Screws
Rust Inhibitor Metal Protector

TOOLS

Circular Saw
Drill with Metal Drill Bits
Hammer
Measuring Tape
Hole Drill Bit
Sandpaper
Tin Snips
Scissors
Construction Gloves
Safety Glasses
Painter's Tape

RECIPE

STEP 1: Start by spraying your corrugated metal sheets and sheet metal with rust protector, and let dry completely. This will protect your sheets from rusting in the future. Maintenance is key with these sheets, so it's smart to spray them every few years.

STEP 2: Once dry, take exact measurements of your walls and cut your corrugated metal sheets to size using your circular saw. Make sure to wear your safety glasses as well as a thick pair of construction gloves. The metal can be sharp.

STEP 3: Measure the exact location of your shower knobs. Using the hole drill bit, predrill your holes. You will be putting the fixture on after the metal is installed.

STEP 4: To protect the corners of the walls, tuck metal flashing at a ninety-degree angle into the corners so it fits snug. Adhere with metal screws and a few dabs of silicone.

STEP 5: After you've installed the flashing to the corners, install the corrugated metal sheets to the walls

continued

using pole barn screws. (The sheets will go right over the flashing.) Space the pole barn screws every foot horizontally and approximately every two or three feet vertically.

STEP 6: Once your panels are installed, seal the plumbing and all the cracks at the seams by running a bead of clear silicone along them to keep them waterproof.

STEP 7: Finally, adhere your vertical trim to the sides with Liquid Nails to finish them off. After your vertical panels have dried, run a thin piece of sheet metal to the top and bottom, adhering with Liquid Nails. You may have to use tape to hold it while it dries.

DEFOREST ARCHITECTS' DESIGNER TIP: Be sure to waterproof the substrate behind the siding so that any water that manages to get through will not cause damage.

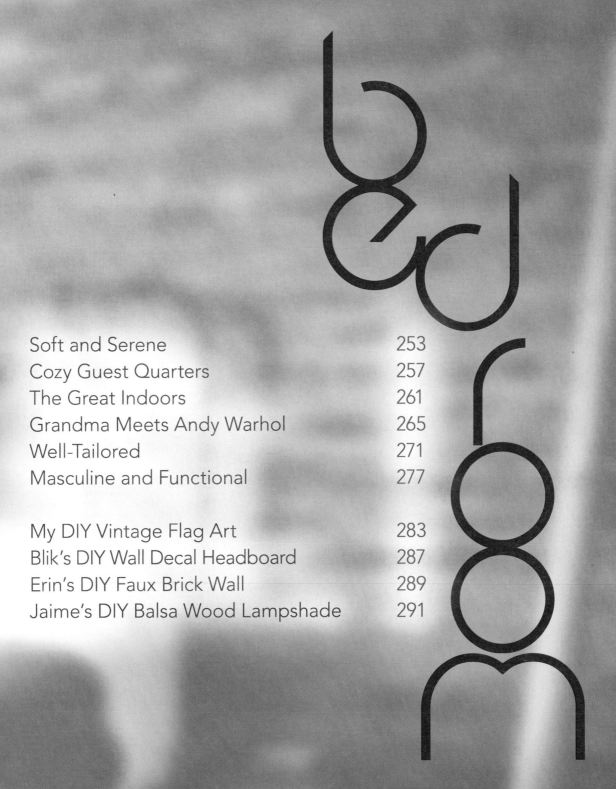

bedroom

BEDROOM

Typically, the bedroom is where we spend most of our time. It's where we go when we want to escape and relax. The trick to making your bedroom feel like your own personal getaway is layering linens, lighting, colors, and textures in a way that's pleasing to your eye. Ultimately, the way these elements relate to each other in the bedroom can affect your mood the moment you walk in. When imagining how you want this room to feel, think about what makes you happy and comfortable.

FOR A RELAXING BEDROOM

- Assess the overall anatomy of the room. Where is the best view? Are you making the most of your space? Is there too much clutter? Not enough surface space? Bad lighting? You may be surprised. Sometimes if you add one piece or replace the bedding, the entire room can take on a whole new life.

- Use color to set the mood of your bedroom. Choose neutral colors for your walls and bedding you believe to be calming. You can punch up the color with a vivid chair, pillow, or piece of art. For a soft monochromatic feel, pick a color on a swatch and then incorporate the color one tone up and one tone down. Using these three colors will provide consistency. If you love darker saturated hues for the walls, downplay the bedding using neutral colors, which will ground the room and keep it from becoming overwhelming.

- Since the bed is the focal point of a room, use that as your starting point. Choose a headboard and a bed frame that best reflect how you want the room to feel. As a general rule:

  - Wood headboards generally feel more rustic and masculine.

  - An upholstered headboard can soften up a space.

  - An ornate headboard can add glamour and detail to a room.

  - A metal frame can feel a little more rustic and/or industrial.

  - A four-post bed can balance out a high ceiling.

  - Smaller rooms typically pair well with platform beds.

- Textiles are so important in your bedroom. When choosing bedding, it's all about layering and avoiding matching bed sets. A mixture of linens adds a feeling of casual elegance. When in doubt, opt for a white duvet, white sheets, and a white bed skirt. For a pop of color, add a throw and decorative pillows. And remember, thread count matters. The higher the better. If there is one place to splurge, this is it. Also, pay attention to what your sheets are made of. Cotton polyester blends tend to be stiffer, while Egyptian cotton sheets will be softer, even at a lower thread count.

- Storage in a bedroom is a luxury. A good option for a large room is an armoire. It offers plenty of storage and can complement the scale of the room. A low chest of drawers and a highboy are great for smaller spaces; however, a low dresser can be a magnet for stuff. Electing for a tall dresser eliminates the temptation to put everything on top of it. Also consider other potential hidden areas for storage. One of my favorites is a box spring with drawers. Once the bed is made, the drawers become completely invisible.

- Side tables are fun accessories that also serve a purpose. Mix and match bedside tables for an eclectic feel. You can also mix and match side tables that are from the same era or opt for a writing desk on one side and a table on the other. If you prefer something a bit more symmetrical or need more storage, choose a table with drawers. For smaller spaces, leggy side tables can open up the space and make it feel less cramped.

- When incorporating lighting in your bedroom, think in layers. Look for lighting that's pleasing and functional at the same time. It can also be visually appealing to use several light sources at lower wattages. Try to avoid all overhead lighting, unless it's a chandelier on a dimmer. Overhead lights tend to be harsh and uncomfortable. Use table lamps on either side of the bed for task lighting or swing arm sconces that will free up space on the nightstand. If installing wall sconces, make sure the bulb isn't exposed. For functional lighting around the room, floor lamps in the corners work well and draw your eye around the room.

- Window treatments are a great way to add color to a room. Regardless of the room size, they should be hung ceiling to floor to play up the height of the room. For added elegance, allow the window treatments to puddle on the floor. Adding a blind and a drape is a good way of layering and varying textures.

- Rugs under your feet can be an added luxury. Go for high pile for softness or a flat weave for something more traditional. Also make sure the rug is big enough. It should fit completely under the bed itself and extend at least twelve inches on all sides. For a smaller option, use a runner on each side. This can be just as comfortable and a bit less cumbersome.

- If you have the space, a bench at the foot of your bed is a great way to complete your bedroom design. Or use a sofa at the end of the bed to mimic a footboard and supply additional seating. If your space is limited, try a few ottomans, a smaller settee, or even a desk. If you find you have the room for two chairs, make sure you add a small side table to make it look intentional.

- Above all, mirrors are the most essential accessories in a bedroom. Place one behind each nightstand to reflect the light and make the room look and feel bigger, or place a larger leaning mirror against one wall. As functional as they are for dressing, they are imperative for glamour.

Channel your inner DIY and create a bed out of galvanized pipe.

Use an
industrial
chest of
drawers
to bring a
masculine
feel into your
bedroom.

SOFT AND SERENE

Everyone has an idea of the perfect room. This is mine: soft, serene, and comfortable. A sanctuary. I love the feeling of waking up to something so quiet that it feels like I'm in a hotel. The idea for this space was to make it so light and airy that you'd want to curl up and take a nap.

INGREDIENTS

Fur Rug
Gray Wingback Upholstered Bed
Mirrored Side Tables
White Lamps
White Mirrors
Soft White Linen Drapes
Pink Coverlet
Small Metal Chair
Fur Throw
Large Piece of Art

RECIPE

STEP 1: To create a serene environment, start with the bed. A wingback bed is a nice option. Its tall headboard gives height to the room while the wings make it feel like the bed itself is being encased. A soft gray is a perfect choice. It's neither masculine nor feminine, so it's easy to switch out your bedding.

STEP 2: Choose simple bedding, such as a silk coverlet, a few pillows, and a faux fur throw. Minimal bedding takes on an understated elegance.

STEP 3: Incorporate mirrored nightstands to add a touch of regency and reflect the texture of the rug. Two inexpensive mirrors placed behind each of the nightstands reflect the light and draw your attention upward.

STEP 4: On the nightstands, white lamps resembling milk glass are a great source of light. The shape is sculptural but not overdone.

STEP 5: Set a small steel chair in the corner of the room. You can add a more substantial chair, but be careful of its scale. You certainly want the bed to be the focal point.

STEP 6: Add an interesting art piece. Use a print on vinyl to bring personality into the space. It goes up like wallpaper but can be removed easily.

STEP 7: Add a cushy floor rug. The soft fur will add texture and feel great under your feet.

Mirrored furniture in the bedroom acts like a gigantic mirror reflection of everything around it. In a small space, use it instead of wood and the room will feel larger.

Forgo the chunky wood bedside table and make a small bedroom feel even lighter by using an open, airy side table.

An understated color scheme, a low bed, and a coverlet with subtle detail create a serene escape.

tengo alas para volar

SEE THE GOOD IN ALL THINGS

Make the most out of a small bedroom by adding a seating area and desk using light furniture pieces that are perfect to the scale of the space.

COZY GUEST QUARTERS

So what do you do with a small, unused space only as wide as a twin mattress? You do as Layla Palmer did and build a well-crafted reading room perfect for overnight guests. Layla used wall-to-wall reclaimed materials, cozy textures, and vertical pieces to create a nook that, with a little DIY, turned into an efficient use of space.

INGREDIENTS

Vintage Floorboards
Custom-Made Plywood Storage Daybed
Preprimed One-by-Two MDF Strips
Flat Baseboard
Crown Molding
White Paint
Chrome Wall Sconce
White Side Table

Storage Boxes
Wicker Baskets
Hanging Pendant
Natural Bedding
Floral Pillows
Black and White Frames
Personalized Artwork
Bright Vintage Tin Accessories

RECIPE

STEP 1: When creating a cottage feel, always look for old materials that can take on a new life. Scour your local salvage shops for wall-to-wall vintage floorboards, which provide a backdrop that has character and depth. Consider this the headboard of the space.

STEP 2: Add one-by-two pieces of primed MDF to the wall as an inexpensive way to dress them up without traditional wainscoting. Painting the trim the same color as the wall makes the side walls just as visually interesting as the back wall.

STEP 3: In a room this small, a built-in daybed looks more like a sofa. With a little elbow grease and some DIY skills, create a base with open storage underneath. This gives your guests a place to store their things while they visit.

STEP 4: Take advantage of the vertical space by hanging interesting pieces, such as stacked framed photos, a wall sconce, and an eye-catching pendant light.

STEP 5: Place a slightly weathered side table flush against the wall for necessary surface space.

STEP 6: Finally, for the cottage vibe, accessorize with linen throw pillows, wicker baskets, and vintage tin boxes to make the space feel intentionally cozy yet not overstyled.

In a small bedroom forgo the standard dresser and choose something, such as an armoire, to house all your incidentals.

Accentuate slanted ceilings and interesting lines with stripes.

Take a Roman shade all the way to the ceiling or create a wall of drapes behind the bed. Your eye will automatically travel up, giving the room the illusion of more space.

THE GREAT INDOORS

I couldn't think of a better title for this room! That's exactly how I feel when I see Percy and Tara's modern cabin bedroom design. The rustic nature of the lath warms the walls with brown and gray tones, and the army blanket on the bed is a perfect accessory. The use of salvaged building materials is a great example of how to find a new life for someone's discarded pieces and make them work in the most fitting ways.

INGREDIENTS

Reclaimed Lath Wood

Iron Bed Frame

Army Blanket

Crisp White Sheets

White Shag Rug

Vintage Wooden Ladder

Throw Blanket

Screen-Printed Poster

Vintage Egg Crate

A Few Good Books

RECIPE

STEP 1: Get your hands on some lath, which is used in building construction. Sadly, most people usually throw lath away, so keep your eyes peeled for demolitions and renovations. No need to prep the wall; lath covers a multitude of sins. But do snap a chalk line every one to two feet to keep things level as you go. Using a brad nail gun or small finishing nails and a hammer, hang the lath one row at a time, cutting to length as needed and taking care to stagger the seams.

STEP 2: Install a great bed frame. A vintage iron frame creates a beautiful centerpiece for the room while keeping with the rustic nature of the space.

STEP 3: In a room with an eye-catching backsplash like this, add simple linens. Here, crisp white sheets pair nicely with a vintage army blanket and add to the cabin vibe.

STEP 4: Scour flea markets to find great accessories and vintage pieces. Boxes and crates make for cheap, simple bedside tables. An old wooden ladder serves double duty as wall décor and creative storage for extra blankets. This is also a great place to inject a little pop of color if the mood strikes.

STEP 5: Use artwork, such as this framed screen-printed poster, to add a modern punch to the vintage look.

STEP 6: Keep your styling simple. You've created a little cabin getaway, so try to keep it relaxing and clutter free. A few vintage books, a rolled-up map in the corner, or other little vintage finds are all you need to personalize the room.

Choose colors that make you relaxed and happy in your bedroom.

Go for something interesting on your ceiling that you can appreciate. Stencils dress up a ceiling and give it character.

Hang a chandelier that represents the style of the room. Wood beads give an exotic feel to an ethnic design scheme.

A swing arm lamp in a bedroom can give you more surface space on the nightstand and works as the perfect illumination for reading.

Hard floors scream for rugs. Mix up your patterns and shapes for more of an eclectic feel.

GRANDMA MEETS
ANDY WARHOL

Here is our lesson in layering! Sasha Emerson and I worked in a homeless women's shelter, each of us taking a room to redesign. The idea was to create a space where each occupant could feel like she was at home. Sasha's room blew me away! As a stylist and interior designer, she created a perfectly layered space with texture, color, and pattern, which is hard to do. The trick, she said, was to use a "prescribed palette," which is simply choosing five to six colors and staying within that vein. She kept a neutral wall, sticking with prints that have the same overall graphic and floral tone and chose bits of black to make the color pop. This room is a great lesson in how pattern, color, textures, and neutrals can live harmoniously in one space. Sasha said, "If this room were a recipe, it would be fruit tart or a strawberry shortcake. Something your grandmother would make. Fun, cozy, playful, and whimsical." Granny chic at its finest!

INGREDIENTS

Custom-Made Danish Modern Sofa/Daybed

Bright, Large-Scale Area Rug

2 Wire Chairs

Storage Armoire

Chinese Import Desk and Side Tables

Midcentury-Modern Overhead Lighting

Fabric-Covered Bulletin Board

Handmade Pillows Made from Leftover Fabric

Graphic Black-and-White Wallpaper

Black Chunky Frames

Leftover Wallpaper Samples

RECIPE

STEP 1: Start with a large area rug that encompasses all the colors in the room. This will ultimately be your go-to palette. Choose five to six colors, and stick within those parameters.

STEP 2: In a room that doesn't get a lot of light, go for a neutral wall color to keep the room cozy. This keeps the room from looking overloaded with patterns and makes everything feel more cohesive.

STEP 3: Wallpaper one wall in a neutral black-and-white graphic to add pattern without overdoing it.

STEP 4: In a small room, you need to be aware of how the space is used. Double-duty furniture is imperative. Instead of choosing a typical twin bed, go with a daybed/sofa combo. If it's in your budget, have one made to fit your space. This also gives you the creative freedom to play with the shape to inject personality into the space with your upholstered pieces.

continued

STEP 5: To prevent every piece of furniture from being the same scale and size, skip the traditional dresser and add a bookshelf armoire to double as the dresser. The armoire will balance the small room and give it height.

STEP 6: Add light, airy wire chairs reupholstered with scrap fabric to act as a good architectural element of the space.

STEP 7: Emphasizing functionality, bring in a pop of color with a desk, like this turquoise one. Choose pieces from a Chinese import store like the side tables and desk to add color and incorporate exotic shapes into the space.

STEP 8: Make instant art with scrap wallpaper and textiles. To balance the varying patterns, choose ones that all have the same underlying principle, such as a graphic print, floral, or color, and try to keep all the frames the same. Traditionally, white or black chunky frames in varying sizes work best.

STEP 9: Layer with caution to create a sense of harmony. Try to stay within five to six colors, and add neutrals. Choose fabrics that all carry the same theme. If you're going for the look of this room, choose patterns that have movement but all have the same underlying whimsical feel. To tie everything in, also consider using a print on more than one item in your space. Upholstering the bulletin board with the same fabric as the pillow on the opposite side of the room balances the space.

STEP 10: Choose lighting based on the mood you want to create, and be sensitive to your light sources. If you're going for the cozy feel, light the room appropriately. A midcentury-modern overhead provides a soft light, while small lamps add task and ambient lighting.

SASHA'S DESIGNER TIP: Making things by yourself can save you money. Scrap wallpaper and fabric can make great wall art. If you don't have enough leftover wallpaper to do a whole room, you can opt for one wall instead. Anything can become art. Framed advertisements or menus can be a quick and easy DIY art piece too!

Take advantage of a nook. A dresser, mirror, and chandelier are turned into a functional vignette without impeding on floor space.

Use a stag head to show off your baubles.

Instead of throwing away your grandparents' old furniture, repurpose it or repaint it.

When you have a large wall with a bold graphic print, stick with two or three colors in the room. This will create balance and give it a classic, uniform look.

WELL-TAILORED

Think of a well-made suit. It's structured, coordinated, and comfortable. When designing for my client Graeme, I wanted him to have that same look and quality in his master bedroom. With simple pieces in rich materials, I gave him layers of style that he could live in.

INGREDIENTS

Dark Blue-Gray Upholstered Headboard

Chrome Side Tables

White Work Lamps

Dark Wood Dresser with Chrome Pulls

Mercury Glass Lamp with a Black Shade

Gray Velvet Drapes with Black Rods

Black-and-White Artwork

White Crisp Bedding with Striped Pillows and Soft Throws

Fig Leaf Tree

RECIPE

STEP 1: Tried and true colors always work well for a tailored masculine bedroom. Shades of blues, blacks, grays, and whites effortlessly transition into one another. Start with a blue backdrop when painting your walls. For a color that feels less boyish, go for blues with hints of gray. In any light, they will look masculine.

STEP 2: Comfort should take center stage even in a masculine abode. Add a large upholstered headboard, low footboard, and side rails with clean lines and piping as the largest piece in the room. An upholstered footboard and side rails will make the bed look more finished and eliminate the need for a bed skirt.

STEP 3: Hang gray velvet drapes for depth and luxury. The less frill here, the better. The plush texture is just enough.

STEP 4: A dark wood lowboy dresser with modern chrome pulls provides storage and gives you an added surface space. With a low dresser, you can hang artwork above the piece and keep all the furniture in the room the same height.

STEP 5: Add nightstands on either side of the bed in chrome to reflect the lamps and mimic the mercury glass lamp and chrome pulls on the dresser.

STEP 6: Purposely placed lighting is key. Flank the bed with white work lamps that act as table lamps. Simple yet architectural, these are perfect reading lights. To illuminate the other side of the space, use a mercury glass table lamp on the dresser. A black shade makes it more masculine.

continued

STEP 7: Mix and match your bedding. Keeping the bedding white and crisp was a necessity for Graeme. So to satisfy my need to mix it up, I incorporated a classic white-and-blue striped set of pillowcases, a large stripe throw pillow, a knitted throw at the end of the bed, and a plush faux fur throw for more texture.

STEP 8: Incorporate life into any space, even in a bedroom. A large fig tree in a large, round vessel accentuates the height and freshens up the space.

STEP 9: Keep the artwork consistent. Two small black-and-white photos flank the bed, while a larger print in a white contrasting frame makes a statement above.

Disguise an old headboard by draping a scarf around it. It's so versatile! Go for vibrant and colorful one season and soft and subdued the next!

Instead of tiebacks, use a simple black ribbon to tie off your drapes.

Create an exotic enclave with ornate textiles, rich colors, and intricate patterns.

For extra storage and a place to sit, set a trunk at the end of the bed. You'd be amazed how much you can fit into it.

MASCULINE AND FUNCTIONAL

I adore Tommy Chambers but loved him even more when I saw this bedroom. I love his approach to design. He believes in incorporating heirloom furniture, collecting art, making furniture out of reclaimed construction material, and tucking your bed into the corner for more floor space. Creative and functional!

INGREDIENTS

Woven Reed Wallpaper
Family Heirloom Dresser
Leather Headboard
Reclaimed Lath Side Table
Oak Bed Frame
Task Lighting
Shearling Rug
Collected Art

RECIPE

STEP 1: Give texture and depth to your walls with woven reed wallpaper. As an added benefit, this texture virtually conceals nail holes, so you can freely change art without a trace.

STEP 2: With limited floor space, consider tucking your bed into the corner. For an easy DIY project, create a headboard that hangs on the wall with a cleat. Wrap two pieces of wood with batting, upholster with leather, and incorporate detail with nail heads. It'll give the bed a resting spot and look like a sofa once it's in the room.

STEP 3: Cherish and use your heirlooms. This dresser was passed down from Tommy's great-grandparents. The bones and structure are amazing, and it'll last a lifetime.

STEP 4: Incorporate something on the floor that is plush and elegant. A shearling rug is great for texture and comfort.

STEP 5: Use old construction materials in new ways. A redwood bedside table made from reclaimed lath is perfect in scale and size for the space. Add a small sculptural task light that pairs nicely with the table.

STEP 6: Incorporate artwork that reflects who you are. Stick with a few styles of frames to mix up the look and keep it interesting.

STEP 7: Lastly, give the room some visual weight with a punch of color on the bed. The orange here makes the look richer, gives it a gentlemanly vibe, and brings the space to life.

Make a small space convertible by tucking the bed into the wall when you aren't using it.

Create space in a bedroom with a modern low-slung platform bed.

For an exotic sea of blue, go for a large coverlet to match the stenciled ceiling.

Decorate the lower half of a slanted wall with a collage of black-and-white photos all of the same subject matter. .

Every room should have a statement piece. Here a black dresser with ivory inlay is so gorgeous that you wouldn't need much more.

Monogrammed pillows give that added sweet touch to the bed. For a more masculine feel, change up the font to block print.

Pair a stack of vintage trunks with a leather-tufted headboard for a masculine feel.

Have fun with your textiles. They are the easiest things to change out. Mix and match colors and patterns for a livable space.

MY DIY VINTAGE FLAG ART

I love flea markets and thrift stores. I could shop thrift stores all day. This piece is why I get up and go. I found this vintage American flag while walking through the Rose Bowl Flea Market. Twenty dollars later, this came home with me! For an additional ten dollars, we have a very American art piece!

INGREDIENTS

Vintage American Flag
2 Pieces of One-by-One Pine*
4 Wood Screws
Brass Upholstery Nails

*Or enough to create a box around the flag

TOOLS

Chop Saw or Handsaw
Drill
Tape Measure

RECIPE

STEP 1: Measure the length and width of your flag. Cut four pieces of pine to create a box around the back of the flag.

STEP 2: Screw together the frame at each of the four ends.

STEP 3: Attach flag with upholstery nails.

A hutch and a desk in a bedroom provide extra storage and surface space. Line the hutch with baskets to store all your little belongings.

Occasional tables are small enough to be pulled out when you need them.

BLIK'S DIY WALL DECAL HEADBOARD

Wall decals are so much fun! They can easily be put up and removed, and they look great in any room. My favorites are the Blik headboards. They're perfect for renters and people who like to change around their décor. You can certainly skip the bulky headboard when you have one of these!

INGREDIENTS

Cleaning Supplies
Smooth Nonporous Surface

TOOLS

Scissors
Squeegee
Plastic Spatula
Thumb Tack
Painter's Tape

RECIPE

STEP 1: In order for the decals to stick, you need a smooth, dry, and clean surface. Grab a dry cloth and give your surface a quick wipe down.

STEP 2: To avoid designer's remorse, tape your decals onto your surface before removing the backing. Step back and admire. If you like what you see, then go for the gold. Depending on your pattern, you may need to cut loosely around the decals so you can have complete freedom to arrange them as you wish.

STEP 3: Now it's time to shift the weight of your decal to the transfer tape. Lay your design on a hard surface, graphic-side-down. Firmly rub over the entire backing with a squeegee, your hand, a credit card, or rubber spatula. Don't hesitate to give it some gusto.

STEP 4: Start at one corner and slowly peel away the paper backing with a rolling action. Some intricate patterns may want to stick to the backing; simply stop peeling, roll back a bit, and re-press the decal onto the transfer tape.

STEP 5: Hold two corners of the transfer tape (with decal, of course) and stick it to your desired surface. Smooth one edge onto the surface first to avoid wrinkles and bubbling. Continue firmly smoothing out the tape all the way down. Ask for help if the image is bigger than you can handle.

STEP 6: Now that you've applied your graphic, it's time to remove the tape. Start at one corner and slowly roll it along your surface. If any part of the decal sticks to the tape, simply stop pulling, roll back a bit, re-press the graphic onto the surface, and continue peeling away slowly.

STEP 7: Bubbling may occur after the graphics are applied. Simply take a thumbtack or needle and poke the bubbled area a couple of times; then smooth it out with your hands.

STEP 8: When you are ready for a new look, removing is simple. If you applied your graphics to a less porous surface like glass, blow-dry (on low heat) to warm it up. This will release the adhesive and make it even easier to peel off. Poof! Back to new.

ERIN'S DIY FAUX BRICK WALL

I was recently living in Chicago, where my apartment had an entire exposed brick wall. Every day I got a chance to look at masonry that was over one hundred years old. It was just marvelous. The downside to this beautiful wall was that it was very cold. Erin, however, created the same look but with faux brick panels. Here she gives us her tutorial on how you can get this look at home, minus the draft!

INGREDIENTS

Faux Brick Panels
Liquid Nails
Joint Compound

TOOLS

Jig Saw
Circular Saw
Nail Gun and Nails
Tape Measure
Helper

RECIPE

STEP 1: Measure the wall/area that you are covering with brick. The faux brick panels are four-by-eight feet and can be purchased at a few hardware stores.

STEP 2: Use your circular saw and jig saw to cut your brick panels. Make sure you measure accurately and include cutouts for the switches and outlets on your wall.

STEP 3: Work your way from one side of your wall to the other. Apply a generous amount of Liquid Nails to the backs of your panels. Have someone help you hold each panel in place while you secure the panels with your nail gun. Secure the panels with a nail every twelve inches vertically and horizontally.

STEP 4: Continue this process until your entire wall/area is covered. Let the panels sit for at least a few hours to ensure the Liquid Nails is adhered and dry.

STEP 5: Apply the joint compound to the grouted areas on the panels. This process is meant to be imperfect and look slightly sloppy. Use your finger to apply the compound to all of the darker/black grouted areas by simply scooping it up and gliding it on.

STEP 6: After the grouted areas are completely dry, add the smeared effects. Use a mud spatula to get this look. Apply a generous amount of the joint compound to your spatula and choose an area on your brick panel where you want more texture. This step is also meant to be imperfect, so just layer it on and apply more if you want it thicker.

STEP 7: To finish up, you can use joint compound to fill in any remaining gaps, spaces, or holes. Don't worry about the small imperfections. Apply the compound to the spaces between your panels and the walls or molding.

JAIME'S DIY BALSA WOOD LAMPSHADE

I love to custom-make my own lampshades. It's an easy way to match your décor. Jaime's custom shade is great because it uses an unexpected material: balsa wood. Even though it looks intricate, it only takes three easy steps! Who wouldn't love that?

INGREDIENTS

Lampshade
Super-Thin Balsa Wood Strips

TOOLS

Glue Gun and Glue Sticks
Hair Dryer

RECIPE

STEP 1: Line the top and bottom edges of the shade with strips of balsa wood. Adhere with a glue gun.

STEP 2: Add pieces willy-nilly! Tuck the ends into the pieces on the top and bottom edges and wrap in a manner that leaves a little space and isn't completely flat against the shade. Keep adding! Keep tucking! The goal is to have all the ends tucked in.

STEP 3: Check for loose ends, and apply glue to adhere. You can remove any wispy glue strands by blowing them with a hair dryer.

Office

OFFICE

Some people have the luxury of dedicating a whole room to their business, while others use their kitchen table or a corner desk. Regardless of the space you're using, it should be outfitted with organizational necessities while maintaining an upbeat sense of style that doesn't scream *office*. To do that, fill the space with things you find inspiring enough to elicit creativity, and never, ever sacrifice style. The truth is, there are no rules here. Having fun designing this space should be the first order of business!

RECIPE FOR A PRODUCTIVE OFFICE

- Assess the space. Ask yourself the following questions: Will I use the office for business or personal responsibilities? Do I need a place to house my computer, printer, and papers, or will a small workstation tucked into a corner be sufficient? What kind of space do I have to work with? Will I entertain clients? All of your answers will give you a pretty good idea of what you'll need from your space.

- Start with the position of your furniture. If you're going to sit at a desk for hours at a time, take advantage of the best view. If you can, position your desk in a direction that will inspire you. Take advantage of the view outside your window: the garden or urban landscape, for example. You want to feel stimulated while you work.

- If your office is in a corner of your living room or bedroom, make sure it's well lit and has a comfortable chair that's stylish and also matches the overall décor of the space. You want it to blend with the rest of the room when it's not being used as a home office. Choosing a secretary desk with a flip-down tabletop or an armoire is a great way to conceal papers and other office supplies behind closed doors.

- If your home office is also your guest room, multifunctional pieces may be necessary. Using a desk as a nightstand works well in a small space, and using baskets and colorful boxes can add texture and color while hiding all your unsightly bills. Try to skip the office chair here and go with something that matches the overall décor to keep everything in the room consistent with a guest room space. Visitors can get uncomfortable if they feel like they're spending the night in your office. Another solution is a roll-down shade or a curtain that you can attach to a bookcase to hide the desk when guests visit.

- Dual desks work well when you have to accommodate more than one person in an office. If you're on a budget, a simple tabletop propped on a few filing cabinets can do the trick, or you can even try a console pressed against a wall. For a larger space, you may want to use a dining table. A communal table looks much more casual and abandons the office vibe.

- Storage is key to staying organized. Papers multiply. Shelves are great for keeping things at arm's length while you are working. And storage pieces on wheels can be tucked away under your desk or in a closet when you aren't using them.

- Floor-to-ceiling bookcases create a library feel. Investing in storage boxes, baskets, and bins to hide paperwork is crucial to dressing up the bookcase and making sure everything has a home. Also remember to do some artful editing with your bookcase. Keeping books color-coordinated or picking the most stylish and putting them out front will ensure your bookcase always looks amazing.

- If your home office gets frequent client visits, make sure you have ample seating. A sofa or upholstered chairs work well and make the room more stylish.

- Lighting is imperative to productivity, but you don't have to use a desk lamp just because it's an office. Opt for a table lamp for more of a casual feel, and incorporate floor lamps and overhead lighting. Pendant lighting or chandeliers add a bit of theatricality and architectural detail.

- Cords can distract from the overall look of the space and tend to appear cluttered and disorganized. To avoid this, always go wireless with your computer and printer. To keep all other cords neat, cord covers are a must.

To camouflage all your paperwork, install ceiling-to-floor panels. A black-and-white graphic stripe makes it fun.

For an instant office, stencil a nook and add some shelves and a chair.

To prevent the space from looking too "office-y," substitute the overstuffed and gaudy office chair with a designer chair.

ARTFULLY ECLECTIC

Amber Lewis is a designer after my own heart. I love all the spaces she creates. She incorporates her love of DIY projects and budget-friendly materials with her very Bohemian-modern design sensibility to create rooms that are affordable, comfortable, and amazing. Good news, though: you don't have to be an avid DIYer to create this functional and affordable office.

INGREDIENTS

DIY Fabric Corkboard
DIY Task Lamp Sconce
DIY Desk
Retro Chair
Graphic Desktop Accessories
Curtain
Greenery

RECIPE

STEP 1: Build your own desk for a fraction of the cost. Buy three filing cabinets, and adhere two tabletops to the top of them. It's a built-in custom desk at a fraction of the cost. Bring in two retro chairs to add to the overall funkiness.

STEP 2: Make your own corkboard out of foam core, cork tiles, and fabric. Without a regular corkboard, the office will feel unique and inspiring. On the corkboard, pin anything and everything that inspires you! Recipes, magazine cutouts, pictures, invitations, etc. Then group everything by color.

STEP 3: Install built-in sconces over the corkboard. They provide great light and add an industrial element to the office. Similar ones can be easily purchased, but to save money you can repurpose task lamps into sconces.

STEP 4: Desktop accessories don't always need to match. It's actually better if they don't! Use cute bowls for paper clips and rubber bands and a tray for a catchall.

STEP 5: Make sure you have ample storage. Magazine boxes are perfect for holding files and notebooks as well.

STEP 6: Forgo the typical closet door, and install curtains curtains with a pop of color and pattern to instantly wake up a neutral room.

STEP 7: Use greenery in almost any room for its height, texture, and color.

AMBER'S DESIGNER TIP: Be creative and find a purpose for objects outside their expected function. An office doesn't have a ton of opportunity for textiles, so drape one of your favorite vintage textiles over the seat. It's comfy when you sit at your desk and looks adorable on the vintage retro chairs.

In a small studio, opt for double-duty furniture by using a console as a great work space.

Punch up the pattern in an office by adding some graphic wallpaper.

Even on a budget, give your office the Hollywood treatment. Chic fabrics, a wingback desk chair, and designer wallpaper remnants can turn any office into the main attraction.

Use graphic prints in an office to make work a bit more fun. Add a chandelier to illuminate a wallpapered ceiling.

FASHIONABLY
BLACK AND WHITE

Corri McFadden is a businesswoman. Owning her own luxury designer consignment service, she needed her space to be the epitome of high style. True to fashion, her black-and-white office looks as though it just stepped off the runway wearing Chanel! In Coco Chanel's words, "I have said that black has it all. White too. Their beauty is absolute. It is the perfect harmony." I have to agree!

INGREDIENTS

Black Paint
White Paint
Ceiling-to-Floor White Curtains
Starburst Mirror
2 Lucite Chairs
Desk Chair
Hanging Designer Pendant Lamp
Side Table
Zebra Hide Rug

RECIPE

STEP 1: The dramatic palette starts with a crisp black-and-white-striped wall to make the room look more spacious. The contrast on your focal wall draws the eye up and down, making the room feel balanced.

STEP 2: Paint the other existing walls black. The dark color gives the illusion that the room's boundaries are blurred, creating a sense of drama and mystery.

STEP 3: Install black floor tiles. The shiny finish gives the room a modern vibe. Larger tiles make the room look bigger.

STEP 4: Lighting is always important in small spaces. Incorporate ceiling-to-floor sheer curtains. In a space this tall, you want to accentuate the height. The sheer curtains allow the sun to peek through, ultimately adding more light to the space.

STEP 5: Punctuate the color with a zebra hide rug. Using another black-and-white print on the floor creates a zone in the office.

STEP 6: Instead of a bulky desk, bring in a sawhorse-style desk. The reflective glass top seems weightless in the space.

continued

STEP 7: For the jewelry of the office, bring in two Lucite chairs. The translucent nature of the chairs allows the sun to shine though, making them almost disappear. A large sunburst mirror on the focal wall reflects the light and bounces it around the room.

STEP 8: Last but not least, add one splurge piece. A designer pendant lamp, mimicking the look of a corset, is used as task lighting.

OFFICE STARTERS AND SWEET TOUCHES

Concrete wire mesh holds up a laminate top. A very inventive desk, I must say!

When paired with a traditional writing desk, a designer Lucite chair enhances the sophistication of the piece.

Add upholstered cushions and a few throw pillows to a bench, and you have a perfect place for clients to sit. Throw on some wheels, and it's mobile.

Keeping the colors bright and cheery makes this room exciting and eye-catching.

NEOTRADITIONAL

Bookcases can truly be a work of art in any space. A well-manicured bookcase speaks volumes. It's not about stacking them to the gills with books and tchotchkes but intentionally styling them. Here in Emily Clark's office, she chose to forgo the small desk for a farmhouse table with more surface space. When paired with upholstered and industrial chairs and backed by layers and layers of books you can't help but get a neotraditional feel.

INGREDIENTS

Farmhouse Table

Comfy Linen Desk Chair

Pair of Tolix Chairs

Large Lantern Pendant and Ceiling Medallion

Floor-to-Ceiling Bookshelves

Ikat Patterned Rug

Ginger Jar Lamp

Lots of Books

Wire Storage Baskets

RECIPE

STEP 1: Custom-made floor-to-ceiling bookcases are the key to creating drama in this space and provide lots of much-needed office storage. For contrast, paint the backs of the bookcases a dark charcoal gray, keeping the rest of the room light.

STEP 2: Instead of a desk, opt for a rustic farmhouse table. It provides a large work space and is a nice contrast to the sleeker elements in the room. Using a distressed piece also means you don't have to worry about scratches from your work materials. An open-legged table allows the bookshelves to be more visible.

STEP 3: A tufted, linen chair provides a comfortable spot to work and softens the lines of the farmhouse table.

STEP 4: Use two Tolix chairs for clients or occasional guests. The metal element adds an industrial feel, and the backs are low enough that they aren't distracting.

STEP 5: Because of the height, the light fixture becomes a focal point of the room. Opt for an oversized pendant to balance out the height and width of the shelves.

STEP 6: Books serve as the artwork for the room. Fill the shelves randomly with colorful spines for a library feel.

STEP 7: Add a colorful rug for a dose of pattern to an otherwise neutral room. Keep the overall design fairly simple, however, focusing on one or two colors.

STEP 8: For task lighting, use a colorful ginger jar lamp on your desk as a great way to bring a pattern into the room.

STEP 9: Add storage. When you have open shelving, inexpensive wire baskets are a stylish option for holding office supplies and other necessary items. They also repeat the industrial element of the Tolix chairs.

A tray catchall and Ikat bowls are a great way to stay organized and add color to your work space.

Create an inspiration board. Attach photos of all the things and people you love. It will keep you motivated, inspired, and happy!

Get inspired by old architecture, and create interest with molding. Paint it the same color as the wall for a modern twist on traditional design.

Every office needs a place for the master of the house. Pull a fur beanbag into the corner so your little friends can spend a day at the office with you.

HIGH STYLE

31

Michelle Adams's office has an eclectic vibe with modern art, midcentury classics, and traditional textiles. It's her perfect selection of hard and soft materials, both masculine and feminine, that brings this whole look together. Combining functional items with bits of glamour proves that you can successfully inject high style into an office space.

INGREDIENTS

White Console
Yellow Lamps
Black and Mercury Glass Lamp
White Round Tulip Table
Leather Office Chair
Black Bamboo Chair with Zebra Upholstery
Black-and-White Floral Chintz Curtains
Black Magazine Holders
Sisal Rug
Large-Scale Artwork

RECIPE

STEP 1: Start with a neutral foundation by adding in a sisal rug. For easier mobility, choose a flat weave.

STEP 2: Hang curtains and artwork that reflect who you are. Even if you don't own the place, this is a good spot to bring in pattern and color and inject your personality. Black-and-white floral chintz adds a modern vibe; if you want more of a traditional look, you could go with a multicolored chintz.

STEP 3: Balance style and function. Use magazine holders in an inexpensive console for contrast and clean, consistent storage.

STEP 4: Bring in a white round tulip table, a midcentury-modern leather chair, and a black bamboo chair reupholstered in zebra fabric. It's important to mix and match the chairs for more of an eclectic feel.

STEP 5: Create an interesting juxtaposition by mixing modern artwork with classic floral chintz. A big print of a single item or person will make the room more intriguing.

STEP 6: To even out the lighting in the room, add pops of color on the console with two bright yellow lamps. For task lighting, forgo the traditional desk lamp and incorporate a table lamp made of mercury and black glass.

STEP 7: Add sculptural items and plants to ease the "office-y" feel and turn this room into its own art piece.

Add nail heads to the sides of a desk. Hardware like this is considered jewelry to interior designers. It dresses up the piece.

O. JOANNES BAPTISTA ANSELMI TEOLOGVS,
ET VICARIVS ABBATIS HVIVS PAROCCHIE,
BENEFACTOR HVIVS CONGREGATIONIS,
ANNA 1797

Vintage luggage serves as great storage and décor in an office.

MODERNIQUE

I love Buckingham Interiors + Design for many reasons. I love that they are masters of mixing styles and eras. Their then-and-now approach to design provides eye candy everywhere you look. Julia Edelman's office engages each visitor with different styles and multiple layers of carefully curated materials, textiles, art, and colors.

INGREDIENTS

Graphic Print Wool Rug
Vintage Glass Cocktail Table
Collection of Framed Art Pieces
Whitewashed Brick Walls
Vintage Side Table
Vintage Candy Dispenser Terrarium
Foundry Parts Console Table
Colorful, Textural Pillows
Refurbished Antique Chairs
Midcentury-Modern Sofa
Antique Swedish Daybed

RECIPE

STEP 1: Start with white walls for a welcoming brightness. This provides a great backdrop to all the contrasting styles, showing off aged pieces.

STEP 2: Ground the room with a large gray-and-white wool rug. This Queen Elizabeth vintage postage stamp print incorporates something old into something new.

STEP 3: Work in your large vintage furniture pieces. A Swedish daybed from the 1850s with its worn original patina and aged elegance works beautifully as a large seating element and is a great conversation piece.

STEP 4: Pair a modern sofa and antique daybed for interesting contrast. With its square shape and midcentury feel, this custom-made crushed-velvet sofa not only ties together other fabrics in the room but also creates a juxtaposition that works so well.

STEP 5: Flank the sofas with a few vintage chairs. These antique chairs were stripped and lacquered in a rich cappuccino color and then reupholstered. To make them even more original, reupholster them in a few different fabrics. A platinum crushed velvet works on the seat, while a shiny metallic abstract floral piece is centered on the back. The look is original by all accounts.

continued

STEP 6: Invest in creative surface spaces. An all-glass vintage coffee table with paper mache vintage dogs tucked inside is both functional and a great conversation piece. A small antique brass midcentury Saarinen table acts as an additional surface for guests.

STEP 7: Incorporate a console behind the sofa. Another DIY project, this console uses a base created from salvage foundry pieces topped with a piece of Danby marble.

STEP 8: Display art by using organized layering and leaning. Here, whimsical artwork paired with antique art from India works because of a singular subject matter.

STEP 9: Accessorize with both old and new pieces. An old nut dispenser turned into a terrarium adorns the console to add a whimsical touch to the space.

JULIA'S DESIGNER TIP: When mixing styles, keep the materials and textures similar for a more cohesive look. Also choose pieces that are in the same color family for an even bigger impact.

MY DIY PAINT CHIP WALL ART

Truth be told, I'm not a very good painter or drawer. When I'm creating art, I like to use other media. I've recently found that a great way to incorporate color into a space is with paint chips. You can make this as big or as small as you want, depending on how much of an impact you want to make in the space. Here, a five-foot piece was made to adorn one very big wall.

INGREDIENTS

Paint Chips
Wood Glue
3 Eight-Foot Two-by-Fours
1 Sheet of Quarter-Inch Four-by-Eight Hardboard

TOOLS

Glue Gun
Chop Saw
Forty-Five-Degree Wood Clamps
Drill
Level
Measuring Tape
Circular Saw or Table Saw
Saw Horses for a Circular Saw
Half-Inch Wood Screws
Four-Inch Wood Screws

RECIPE

STEP 1: Start by creating a frame with your two-by-fours. Figure out your desired length and width of the overall piece and subtract six inches from each side. Ultimately when it's hung you want it to look like it's floating on the wall as opposed to having a border.

STEP 2: Cut the two-by-fours and, using your forty-five-degree wood clamps, screw together the outside wood frame. Measure the inside length, and cut and screw in two center pieces for support. It's best to space them equally.

STEP 3: Next, cut the hardboard to size. You want it to be six inches longer and taller than your wood frame.

STEP 4: After you've cut your hardboard, place in on top of your frame and screw it in.

STEP 5: Using your glue gun, randomly glue your paint chips to the hardboard. Here you can have some fun with the colors and the patterns.

STEP 6: To make a wall cleat, measure between each center support, and cut two two-by-fours four inches smaller.

STEP 7: Using the level, screw the two-by-fours into the wall where you want the art to be hung.

STEP 8: With someone helping you, lift the art piece over the cleats so they are positioned in between the vertical braces and screw from the top down.

KRISTINE'S DIY
OFFICE DRAWERS

32

Storage, storage, and more storage. We can never get enough, especially in an office. Use these drawers that Kristine Franklin made to store small trinkets, business cards, or desk supplies.

INGREDIENTS

Moppe Drawers from Ikea
Brass Plate Holders
Timber Stain
Danish Oil

TOOLS

Sandpaper
Small Picture Nails
Mallet
Paintbrush or Sponge

RECIPE

STEP 1: Turn the drawers around, and use the opposite side to hide the finger cutouts.

STEP 2: Give the corners of the drawers a reasonably heavy sand to round them off a bit, which imparts the illusion of some wear.

STEP 3: Apply two coats of timber stain.

STEP 4: To add a soft luster and enhance the richness of the stain, apply three coats of Danish oil.

STEP 5: Once the oil is dry, attach the pulls using the small picture nails and mallet. Place them a little higher than midway.

STEP 6: The nails, which affix the pulls, will inevitably poke through the rear of the drawer fronts. File them flush, or trim them down prior.

STEP 7: To finish, design some simple antique-style tabs for the cardholders.

LEAH'S DIY GLOBE LIGHT

Great for a dining room, an office, or a kid's room, this fun project takes something that we've all owned at one time and turned it into something else. Leah Moss's globe light is a perfect example of repurposing and reusing!

INGREDIENTS

Pendant Light Kit
Light and Cord Kit
Globe
Paint
Chalk

TOOLS

X-ACTO Knife or Box Cutter
Paintbrush

RECIPE

STEP 1: Using your X-ACTO knife, carefully cut the globe in half along the equator. Most old globes are joined here with only glue or tape, so this takes about two seconds.

STEP 2: Hold the light socket of your pendant light on the top of your globe (north or south pole, depending on which half you're using) and use it as a stencil as you trace around it to mark the spot where it will be inserted.

STEP 3: Using your X-ACTO knife, cut around the circle you just marked. (The lip of the pendant light should cover this area once it's assembled, so this doesn't have to be a perfectly clean cut.) Some globes that were previously on rotating stands have a metal washer-like disc glued on at either pole, so be careful as you cut around it and remove it. If your blade doesn't cut through the globe easily, it probably means that you do have one of these metal discs.

STEP 4: Paint the inside of your globe using whatever color your prefer.

STEP 5: Install the pendant light into the ceiling. (Hire an electrician or go with the plug-in version if you don't know how to switch out the existing feature yourself.)

STEP 6: Fit the light socket through the hole at the top of your globe, screw on the cap, pop in the bulb, and ta-da!

JEN'S DIY FLOATING OFFICE CABINETS

Storage is a luxury, especially in an office where papers can pile up. For added storage, you can always use premade cabinetry, like Jen Ramos did, and retrofit it to your space. New knobs and a surface space on the modern high-gloss doors will give any office a glamorous high-end look.

INGREDIENTS

Premade Cabinets with Rail
One-Inch Poplar Wood Top
Ebony and Dark Walnut Stain
Liquid Nails
Brass Knobs

TOOLS

Drill
Step Stool
Staining Brush and Rags
Level
Measuring Tape

RECIPE

STEP 1: Purchase Ikea Akurum cabinets, thirty-six inches wide by twenty-four inches tall with white, high-gloss Abstrakt doors.

STEP 2: After constructing the cabinet boxes without the doors, hang the rail (Ikea cabinets actually hang on a wall-mounted rail). Cut the rail exactly so that the hardware reaches on both ends. This one was hung with an eight-inch gap under the cabinets, so the rail was thirty-one inches off the ground.

STEP 3: Plan ahead. You will want at least two stud screws per cabinet along the rail, so use a good stud fnder to mark where those go. If you expect to have a lot of weight, you may also want an extra one or two toggle bolts. Be sure to use a good level (either a laser level or a long one).

STEP 4: Once the rail is hung, slide the square nuts into the rail with the screw heads extended. Use a step stool to help balance the boxes as you put each one into position and mount the inner hardware. Leave it slightly loose so you can slide them side to side until they are in position.

STEP 5: For the top, use a one-inch-thick poplar from a local lumberyard and have them mill a piece to fit twelve-feet-one-inch by thirteen feet by one inch (remember that the cabinets are thirteen inches deep with the doors). Have the mill sand it, or do it by hand. The better you sand, the better it will be. Then stain your wood by mixing ebony and a dark walnut so it will be a black brown. Glue it down with Liquid Nails, and then screw from underneath with one-and-one-fourth-inch wood screws.

STEP 6: Using the hinge screws, hang the doors and adjust them until they are level. For the pulls, consider looking online for some that give the piece a high-end feel.

JEN'S DESIGNER TIP: When ordering the cabinets from Ikea, be sure to buy the knob guide: it will help to position them exactly.

TYPHANIE'S DIY LAMPSHADE

I first saw Typhanie's lampshade when we worked together on a charity project last year. I was so impressed. In an effort to tie the lampshades to the rest of the room, she made them! Here she shares her steps for creating this unique piece.

INGREDIENTS

A Nonpleated Lampshade
Newspaper or Craft Paper
Pins
1 Yard of Fabric
Spray Adhesive
Fabric Glue
Ribbon or Cording

TOOLS

Hot Glue Gun
Craft Glue
Pencil
Sharp Scissors

RECIPE

STEP 1: Place the lampshade on its side on the sheet of paper (newspaper or craft paper), lining up its seam with the left edge of the paper. If your shade is wider at the bottom, place it near the bottom of the paper's edge.

STEP 2: Trace the bottom and top edges of the shade with your pencil, slowly rolling the shade as you go until you get back to the seam.

STEP 3: Extend the two lines by an inch, and draw a straight line between them.

STEP 4: Cut out the shape you've drawn. If you want to crease your fabric under for finished edges, cut half an inch outside the lines.

STEP 5: Pin this paper pattern to your new fabric. Carefully cut out the new lampshade cover from the fabric, tracing around the paper.

STEP 6: On your leftover scrap of fabric, test your spray adhesive to make sure it won't cause discoloration or show through on the other side.

STEP 7: Spray the inside of your new fabric with the adhesive. Tip: You can brush on diluted fabric or craft glue instead of spray adhesive.

STEP 8: Carefully place the lamp shade onto the now sticky fabric, lining up the seam with a short edge.

STEP 9: Slowly roll the shade over the fabric a little bit at a time, smoothing the fabric out toward the edges as you go until your new cover is in place.

continued

STEP 10: Trim away any bits of excess fabric that extend above and below the shade. If you cut your fabric generously, use fabric glue to tuck the edges and seam under.

STEP 11: Allow the seam to overlap itself by at least one-quarter inch in case the fabric shrinks a little as it dries.

STEP 12: Trim the bottom and top edges with a ribbon, cord, or fringe, using fabric glue or a hot glue gun to secure it a bit at a time.

STEP 13: Pin the trim in place as you go so it dries in a neat line.

STEP 14: When the adhesive and glue have dried, return your shade to your lamp.

JUTTA'S DIY
PAINTED GLASS JARS

Jutta Rikola's office project gives new life to leftover paints and glass jars that tend to pile up in cupboards. Simple and easy, it's a great office DIY using things that you already own. Use the jars for storing pens, pencils, or office supplies.

INGREDIENTS

Paint
Glass Jars
Lids
Old Newspapers
Spray Paint

RECIPE

STEP 1: The paint should be thick enough to stick to glass but not too thick. If it's too thick, you can dilute it with water or paint thinner, depending on your paint.

STEP 2: Clean and dry the jar thoroughly. Pour in some paint.

STEP 3: Close the lid so you don't get paint all over. Swirl and shake. Twist and turn.

STEP 4: Pour most of the excess paint back in the paint can.

STEP 5: Place the lid on the jar. Leave the jar upside down to drip overnight.

STEP 6: Pour out the remaining excess paint.

STEP 7: If the paint is too thick and you can't pour it all out, you can try to wipe it, but be careful not to remove too much. You don't want clear glass to show.

STEP 8: Wipe the rim clean before the paint dries. If the paint does dry, you may need to scratch it with your fingernails. Place the lid on the jar. Leave the jar upside down to drip overnight.

CONTRIBUTORS

Kelly Edwards is not just another designing diva. This former teen beauty queen is also a do-it-yourself darling with passion for all things self-created. Thanks to her amazing ability to turn a simple space into an innovative interior with only a $1,000 budget, Kelly Edwards has been deemed over the airwaves as the "MacGyver of Design."

The Style Network and HGTV star offers dwellers with decorating dilemmas distinctive design tips, bargain-decorating projects, and total home makeover transformations inspired by personal style and popular trends. Kelly is well-known for her knack at repurposing everyday items into extraordinary collectibles, refurbishing unique home accessories, and crafting recipes for creative cleaning solutions.

No stranger to television, Kelly cohosted one of HGTV's most popular shows, *Design on a Dime*, and recently teamed up with celebrity interior designer Thom Filica to cohost Style Network's hot design show *My Awesome Room*, and became a segment host and design expert on AOL Living. In addition, Kelly has appeared on ABC's *Holiday of Stars*, where she designed former *The Bachelor* star and football analyst Jesse Palmer's bachelor pad for the holidays.

Appearing regularly in national design and decorating magazines, such as *Cosmopolitan*, *Life & Style*, and *Good Housekeeping*, Kelly is also a national spokesperson for Waterpik shower heads, and has been seen in several infomercials for Oreck vacuum cleaners and Cricut. When she's not filming, she travels to speak on design both at home shows and on news stations nationwide, carrying the idea that anyone can design their own home. Kelly speaks to hundreds of homeowners, encouraging them to pick up the power tools and do it themselves. As a self-taught decorator, Kelly believes everyone can master their own personal design one nail at a time. She thinks just having the right recipe may be all they need.

Be in the know on the latest Medallion Press news by becoming a Medallion Press Insider!

<u>As an Insider you'll receive:</u>

· Our FREE expanded monthly newsletter, giving you more insight into Medallion Press

· Advanced press releases and breaking news

· Greater access to all your favorite Medallion authors

Joining is easy. Just visit our website at
<u>www.medallionmediagroup.com</u> and click on
Super Cool E-blast next to the social media buttons.

Want to know what's going on with your favorite author or
what new releases are coming from Medallion Press?

Now you can receive breaking news, updates, and more from
Medallion Press straight to your cell phone, e-mail, instant messenger, or Facebook!

twitter

Sign up now at <u>www.twitter.com/MedallionPress</u> to stay on top of all the happenings in and around Medallion Press.

MEDALLION
P R E S S
medallionmediagroup.com